IMAGES
of America

HENDERSONVILLE

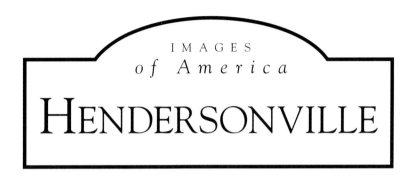

Galen Reuther and Lu Ann Welter

Copyright © 2005 by Galen Reuther and Lu Ann Welter
ISBN 0-7385-4184-2

Published by Arcadia Publishing
Charleston SC, Chicago IL, Portsmouth NH, San Francisco CA

Printed in Great Britain

Library of Congress Catalog Card Number: 2005930278

For all general information contact Arcadia Publishing at:
Telephone 843-853-2070
Fax 843-853-0044
E-mail sales@arcadiapublishing.com
For customer service and orders:
Toll-Free 1-888-313-2665

Visit us on the internet at http://www.arcadiapublishing.com

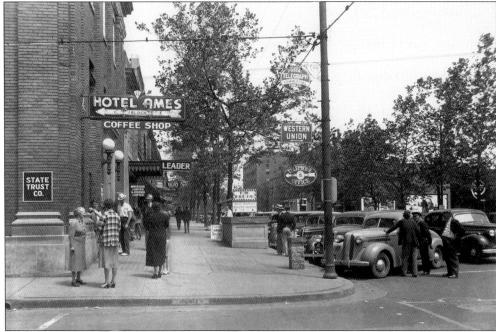

Pictured here is the corner of Main Street and Fourth Avenue West in Hendersonville c. 1940. Seen on this corner is the State Trust Bank building that is now a restaurant. Also visible near the center of the photo is the old entrance to what was an underground shopping area. On the sidewalk, there were glass blocks that allowed light to penetrate underground. (Photograph courtesy Baker-Barber Collection, Community Foundation of Henderson County.)

Contents

Acknowledgments	6
Introduction	7
1. Hendersonville: City of Four Seasons	9
2. Churches and Schools	27
3. Houses and Historic Districts	45
4. Hotels and Boarding Houses	57
5. Business and Industry	69
6. Festivals and the Arts	85
7. Sports and Recreation	95
8. People	107

ACKNOWLEDGMENTS

It has not been an easy task to capture the history and complexity of Hendersonville and its people, but we hope this book will increase your interest and involvement in this very special city. Neither of us is a native North Carolinian, but we have adopted this beautiful area with a passion during the many years we have called it home. We have visited with and spoken to so many wonderful people that it is impossible to thank everyone for opening their photograph albums and relating fascinating stories of days gone by. We have not tried to write the history of Hendersonville but have tried to give a glimpse into its past and of the people and places that make it special.

Many of the photographic images included in this book, though provided by other sources, are part of the Baker-Barber Collection, owned by the Community Foundation of Henderson County, Inc., and held at the Henderson County Public Library. The Baker-Barber Collection was gifted to the Community Foundation of Henderson County by Joseph Egerton Barber in 1993 to provide cultural, educational, historic, and civic enrichment for the community. Persons interested in further information about this collection or specific photographs should contact the Henderson County Public Library.

In addition to our families who have offered continued support during this project, we want to give special thanks to David W. Cooley, Charlie King, Hendersonville Chamber of Commerce, the City of Hendersonville, and the Hendersonville Historic Preservation Commission.

INTRODUCTION

No one really knows precisely when the first settlers came to our region, but enough information has been handed down to provide a sketch of the early years that is presumed accurate. What is now Henderson County was the southern section of Buncombe County. It is not an old area, especially in comparison to the coastal areas of North Carolina, which were settled as early as the 16th and 17th centuries. The scope and size of the beautiful Blue Ridge Mountains and the lack of a large navigable waterway contributed to the area's later settlement.

The land was favored by the Cherokee Indians as a hunting and camping area evidenced by documented stories of meetings on the great flat rock, from which the village of Flat Rock took its name. On the heels of the Cherokees came the earliest settlers. Many of these hardy, industrious men were veterans of the Revolutionary War who had been awarded land grants for their military action and patriotism. These pioneers were searching for land to establish homesteads where they could raise their families and enjoy freedom of religion. Word spread of the lovely weather, clean water, and fertile valleys, so they came by foot, horseback, and ox-driven wagon over the mountains and through the passes from Pennsylvania, Virginia, and New York.

Henderson County was created out of the southern part of Buncombe County in 1838 by the North Carolina Legislature. Leonard Henderson, a native of Granville County in the eastern part of the state, had been chief justice in the Supreme Court of North Carolina in the years just prior to the new county's creation. It appears that the naming of the county was a political understanding. Representatives of the eastern counties were asked to support the new county in return for naming it after the popular chief justice. Chief Justice Henderson never visited the western part of the state.

Locating a site for the county seat proved to be a difficult matter. Horse Shoe was initially chosen as the county seat, and its name was to be changed to Hendersonville. Enormous outcries about the location came from the eastern part of the county because of the distance between them and the proposed county seat. Disagreements continued, and in 1840, the general assembly passed a bill for a vote to decide the matter. The site location was to either be on or near the Buncombe Turnpike or at Horse Shoe on the French Broad River. Once a site was chosen, a town was to be surveyed into lots, streets named, and town limits drawn. The election took place, but meanwhile Judge Mitchell King, an admired early settler with extensive land holdings, offered to give 50 acres, bounded on the south and east by Mud Creek, for the county seat. This land was along the Buncombe Turnpike. In addition to Judge King's land, adjoining 29-acre parcels were given by Col. James Brittain and John Johnson. The town was surveyed, lots were sold, and the city of Hendersonville had its beginning.

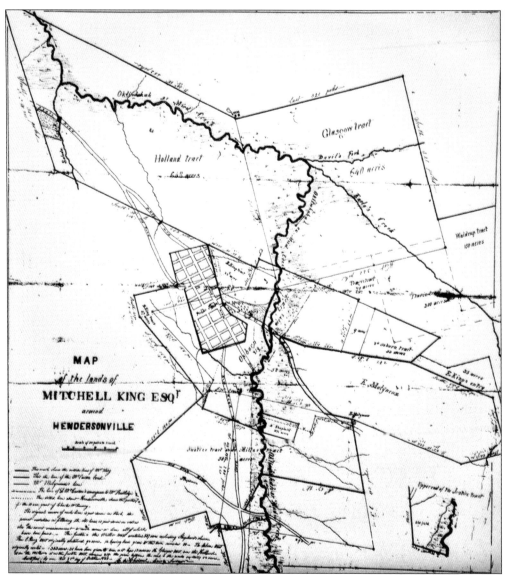

Seen here is a photograph of the original layout of the City of Hendersonville indicating the lands donated by Judge Mitchell King Esq. and adjoining pieces of property. This map can be inspected closely at the Henderson County Courthouse, hanging in the central hall.

One
HENDERSONVILLE
City of Four Seasons

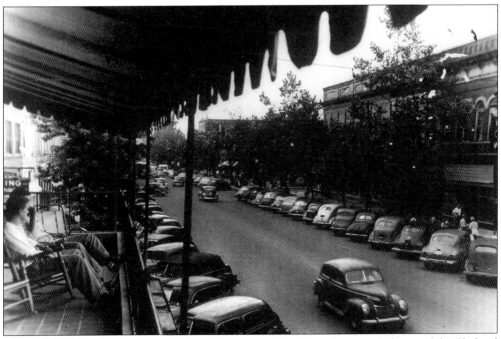

This wonderful c. 1945 picture of Main Street was taken from the open balcony of the Skyland Hotel. Two friends are relaxing in rocking chairs, watching the hustle-bustle of the street. They are looking south toward Fifth Avenue. (Photograph courtesy of Charlie King; Baker-Barber Collection, Community Foundation of Henderson County.)

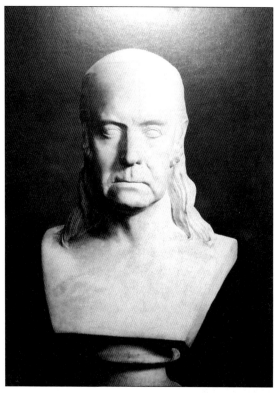

Pictured here is a bust of Judge Mitchell King. Judge King gave 50 acres to establish the county seat. He also donated land for a school. As part of the agreement, the building must always remain an educational facility, or the land reverts to the King family. Judge King was born in Scotland in 1783, immigrated to Charleston, South Carolina, in 1805, and built his home, Argyle, in Flat Rock c. 1830. (Courtesy of Danny Ogletree and Alec King.)

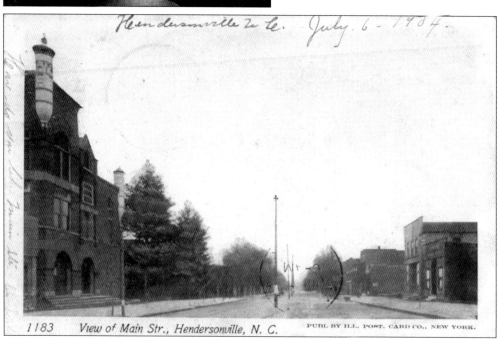

This is a postcard showing the original Hendersonville town hall and opera house. The postcard is dated July 6, 1904. The photograph appears to have been taken just after the building opened. The town hall and opera house dominated the east side of Main Street in the 400 block. The opera house was used for plays, recitals, and one-man shows.

Here is an old picture of a store operated by Hezekiah Elezer "Skin" Drake that stood on the corner of Main Street and First Avenue East. It was a central gathering place for many years. Long considered the first commercial building on Main Street, it also housed the first post office for Hendersonville, an infirmary during the Civil War, the M. M. Shepherd store, and the Baker Art Gallery. (Courtesy of Jeff Miller.)

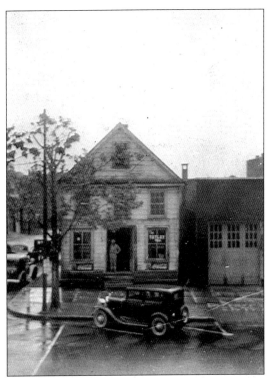

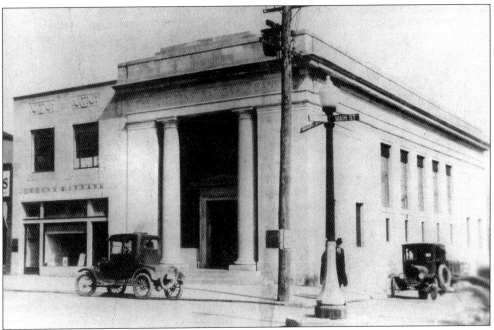

This is a photograph of Citizens National Bank and the Ewbank and Ewbank Building, c. 1920. The bank stands on the corner of Main Street and Fourth Avenue East. The bank building now houses the Genealogical Society and the Mineral Museum. Some time after this photograph was taken, a clock was added to the side of the building. (Photograph courtesy of Charlie King; Baker-Barber Collection, Community Foundation of Henderson County.)

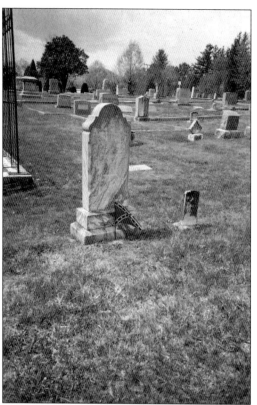

Pictured here are graves of two young men, Watt Bryson, son of William Bryson, and George Mills, an enslaved servant to the Bryson family. Watt Bryson was near Malvern Hill, Virginia, fighting for the Confederacy when Mills, 18 at the time, was sent to take care of him. When Mills arrived, he found his master dead. As promised, Mills brought the body back to Hendersonville, taking many days by wagon and train. Bryson's grave is pictured to the left and is next to Wolfe's Angel in Oakdale Cemetery (see page 33). George Mills grave site, below, is across Highway 64 also in Oakdale Cemetery. Mills became a soldier in the Home Guard and served throughout the war. He was given his freedom and a pension for wartime service. Watt Bryson was first interred at the First Methodist church cemetery. When the city opened Oakdale Cemetery, the graves were moved there, and Mills oversaw, once again, the burial of his friend and former master.

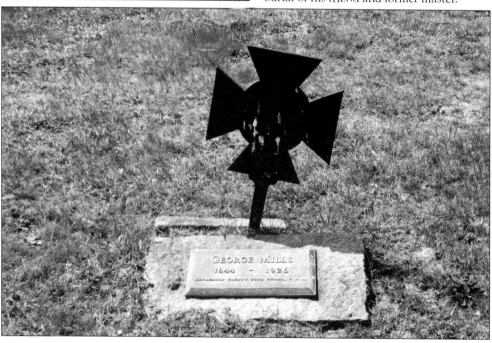

There was tremendous division within families and among friends during the Civil War each seeing justification in their cause. North Carolina was the last of the Confederate states to pass an Ordinance of Secession. This photograph is of a grave in the old cemetery of the Dana United Methodist Church. It marks the resting place of John Young, a soldier of the Confederacy.

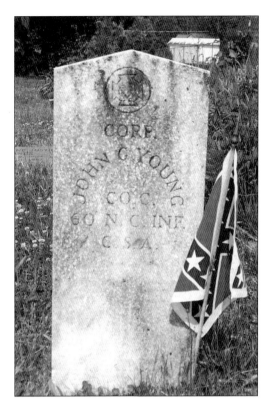

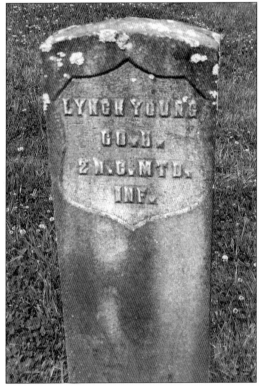

This is a photograph of the grave of Lynch Young, who fought for the Union. He was the brother of John, whose grave is pictured above. There was much heartbreak and hardship during the Civil War. Although Hendersonville did not see battles, as the conflict continued, and deprivation arrived. Luxuries, such as fine fabrics, became scarce and finally disappeared. Confederate currency lost its value. Recovery took a very long time.

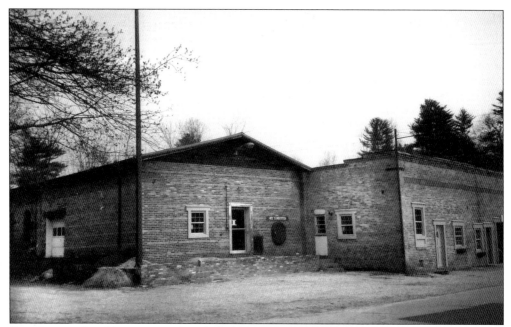

Seen here is the old city ice and coal plant on Whitted Street, owned by Fred Suddeth, and still standing today. The water came into the back of the building and then was frozen, cut into blocks, and sent through the opening at the front of the building. The ramp was raised so ice could go directly onto a wagon. To the right in this picture is the storage building. Ice was also delivered by wagon, pulled by a team of huge horses, and manned by a deliveryman wearing a long leather apron.

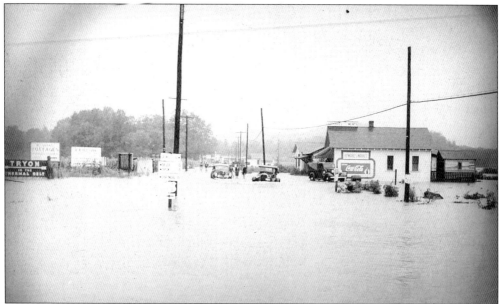

This sight might look familiar to many Hendersonville residents. The view is of the intersection of Route 25 south and 176, Spartanburg Highway. The Fresh Market is now located to the right of the picture and Carolina First Bank is where Howard's Market is pictured here. (Photograph courtesy of Charlie King; Baker-Barber Collection, Community Foundation of Henderson County.)

The cover of a tourist guide, *Day by Day in Hendersonville*, published September 17, 1923, is shown here. It lists 16 hotels, 49 boarding houses, 14 camps, and train schedules between Hendersonville and Asheville, Spartanburg, Cincinnati, and Charleston. It also prints the mail schedule, the movie schedule at the Queen Theater, and names the locations of nine churches. (Courtesy of E. Mark Fender.)

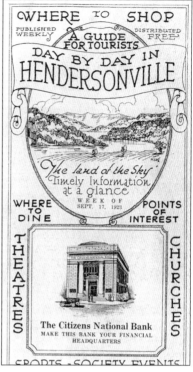

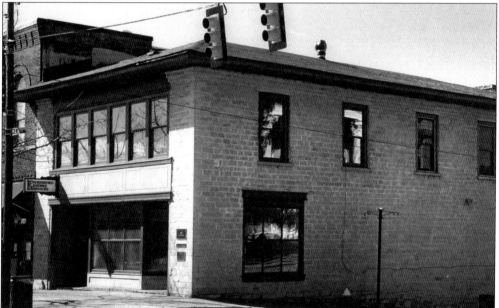

This is a recent photograph of the oldest surviving building on Main Street located on the corner of Main Street and First Avenue West. Built by Col. Valentine Ripley, c. 1847–1848, it has undergone many alterations throughout the years. Colonel Ripley, a native of Virginia, came to Hendersonville c. 1830. He acquired quantities of land and ran the stagecoach from Greenville, South Carolina, to Greenville, Tennessee, and was district commissary under Major Noe during the Civil War.

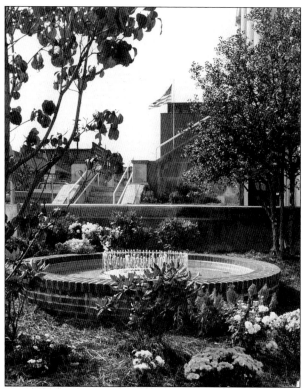

Shown here is a c. 1968 photograph of the fountain and garden installed at Hendersonville City Hall by the Garden Club of Hendersonville in memory of Mrs. Edward Lynn. The fountain completed the landscaping for city hall at the time. The corner of King Street and Fifth Avenue was a visual delight for passersbys for nearly 37 years. (Courtesy of the Garden Club of Hendersonville, Inc.)

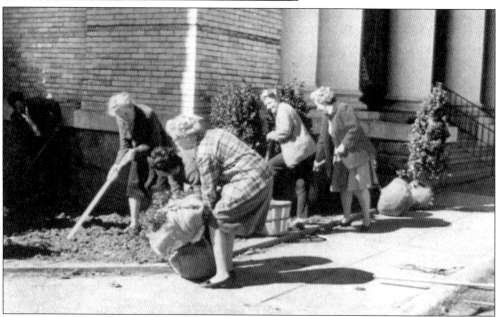

The Garden Club of Hendersonville was formed in 1960, and beautification projects were immediately undertaken. The most industrious project began around 1963—a major face-lift of the Henderson County Courthouse. A notable feature is the pair of spruce trees on either side of the main entrance. Pictured here from left to right are Pat Schell, unidentified, Geneva Butler, Niva Larson, and Dot Franklin. (Courtesy of the Garden Club of Hendersonville, Inc.)

Here is a recent photograph of the old Henderson County Jail. Located in the rear of the historic Henderson County Courthouse, the jail was built on the same site as the first jail that contained "rooms" for criminals, with signs on room doors reading "criminals," "Negroes," "debtors," and "females." In back of the first jail was the whipping post. The last person to be publicly hanged was Lewis Kilgore c. 1886; the gallows were built where Curb Market is today.

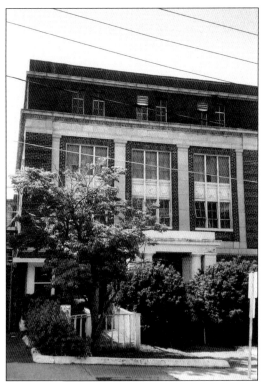

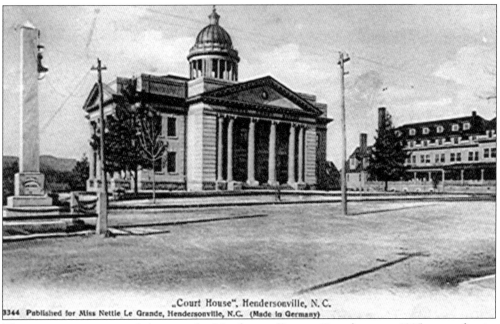

This is a vintage postcard showing the Henderson County Courthouse c. 1905 soon after its completion. This courthouse took the place of the original one on the same site, which served the county from around 1842 to around 1905. The jail was at the back of the courthouse. Notice the Confederate War Memorial in the middle of Main Street. Appearing in the background is the St. John Hotel, which burned around 1915.

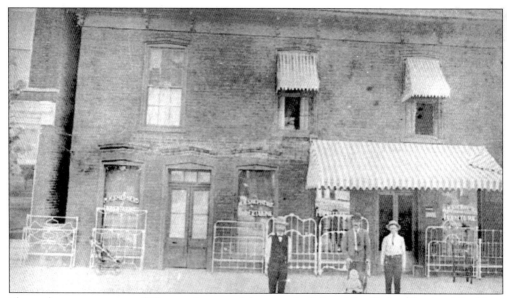

Shown here are two very different pictures of the same building. The Ripley-Shepherd Building at 218 Main Street was built c. 1847 by Col. Valentine Ripley and appeared as it is shown in the photograph above. It was built about the same time Colonel Ripley was building on First and Main Streets, so there is some confusion as to which is the older of the two structures. Beginning c. 1872, this building passed from Ripley through several owners, before M. M. Shepherd and F. G. Hart purchased it c. 1889. Shepherd and Hart opened furniture and mortuary businesses in the building. Tom Shepherd, brother of M. M. Shepherd, acted as manager for several years before buying out his partners and moving the mortuary business to Church Street. The building remains in the Shepherd family to this day and now appears as in the photograph below. It recently won the 2004 best Historic Rehabilitation Project for a North Carolina Main Street Center. (Courtesy of Sue Shepherd Sneeringer.)

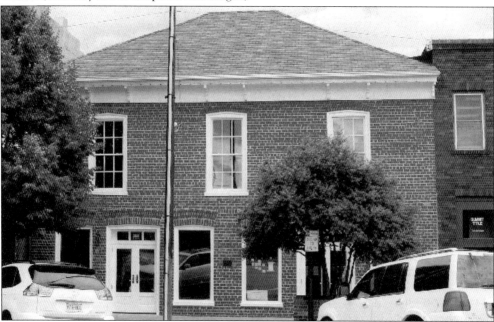

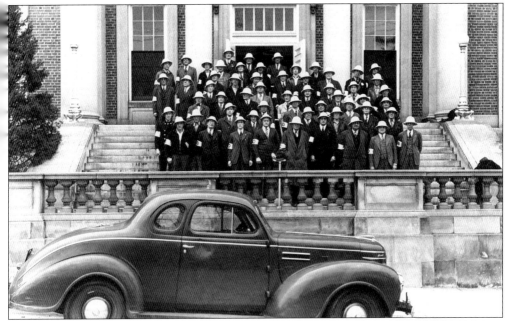

Here is a great photograph of Hendersonville's civil defense team during World War II. Many were air raid wardens who would warn the city in the event of an attack. This picture is taken on the steps of city hall, c. 1943. (Courtesy of Charlie King.)

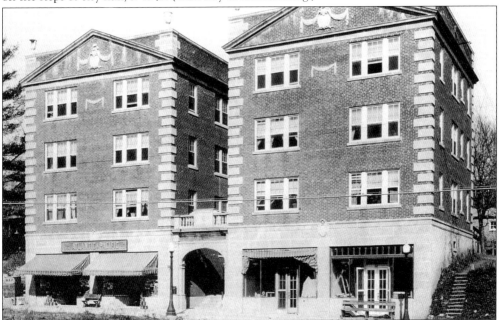

The Maxwell Apartments, designed by Erle Stillwell, were built c. 1920 and were in fact an addition to an existing boardinghouse called the "Dickinson." The Great Atlantic and Pacific Tea Company (the A and P) occupied the street-side first floor of the apartment building. Ralph Martin ran the store, and after the A and P moved to Greenville, he opened the Jax Pax in the same location. (Photograph courtesy of Lynn Blackwell; Baker-Barber Collection, Community Foundation of Henderson County.)

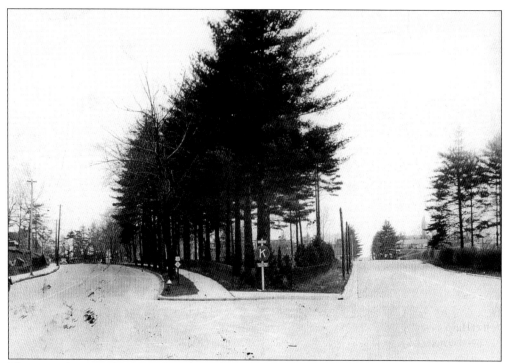

This is a photograph of Boyd Park at the old entrance to Hendersonville coming from the north. The street to the left is Main Street, and to the right is Church Street. King Street did not connect with Church Street at this time. (Photograph courtesy of Hendersonville Chamber of Commerce; Baker-Barber Collection, Community Foundation of Henderson County.)

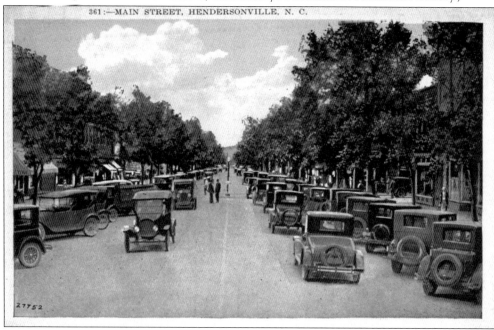

Here is another view of Main Street looking south. This vintage postcard dates from the 1920s. Still visible is the line in the middle of the street where telegraph and lighting poles once stood.

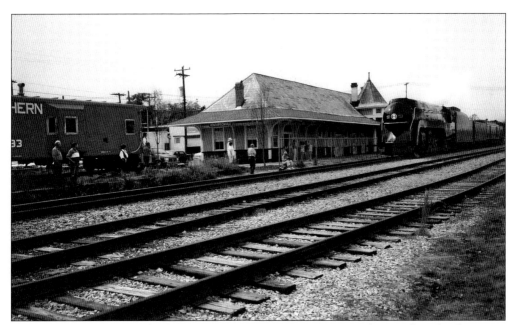

This c. 1994 image is of the last passenger train coming into Hendersonville. The first train arrived here in 1879, and 3,000 people turned out to meet it. The Carolina Special operated from c. 1911 to c. 1968. It went from Charleston, up the Saluda Grade—with help from a "pusher" engine since it is the steepest grade in the United States—through Hendersonville, and on to Ohio. (Courtesy of Andries Jansma.)

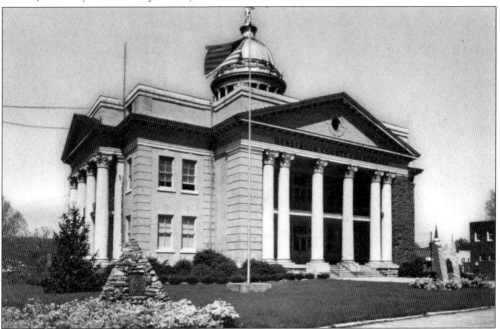

Here is a postcard showing the Henderson County courthouse, as pictured in the 1960s. This photograph was taken shortly after the Garden Club of Hendersonville completed the landscaping. On the left is a monument to Daniel Boone who is often credited with opening passage through the Appalachian Mountains.

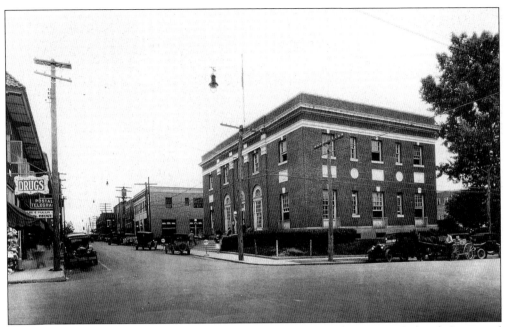

Pictured here is the Hendersonville Federal Building, located on the corner of Church Street and Fourth Avenue. Completed c. 1914, it was the main post office until 1966 when the new post office was built on Fifth Avenue. The Federal Building was designed by local architect Erle Stillwell. (Photograph courtesy of David W. Cooley, and Hendersonville Chamber of Commerce.)

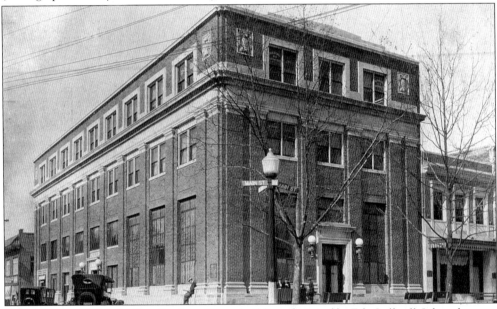

Shown here c. 1923 is the First Bank and Trust building, designed by Erle Stillwell. It later became the State Trust Co., which merged with Northwestern Bank around 1958. It is now offices and a restaurant. Sometime after this photograph was taken, an entrance to the underground was cut through the sidewalk for access to the Teen Canteen and other shops. (Photograph courtesy of Hendersonville Chamber of Commerce; Baker-Barber Collection, Community Foundation of Henderson County.)

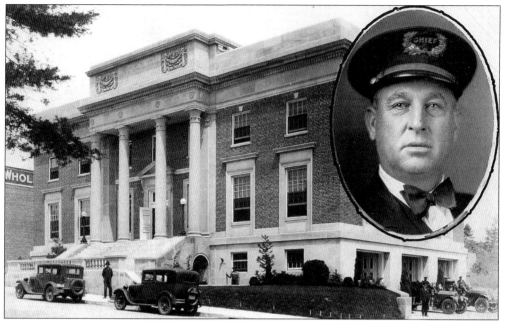

The Hendersonville City Hall, designed by Erle Stillwell, was completed in 1928 and has served the city ever since. In the past, the building housed the city's courtroom, health department, jail, and motor vehicle office. In 2005, the building went through a total renovation that added many modern conveniences and a reception lobby accessible from the parking lot. Chief Otis Powers is pictured in the inset. (Courtesy of Hendersonville Chamber of Commerce.)

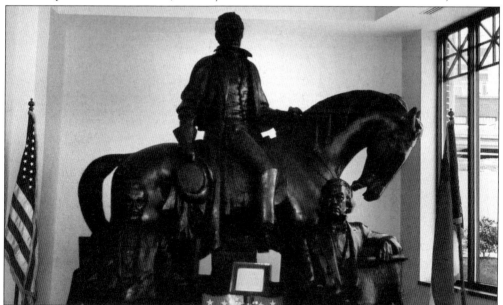

This is a statue of the three North Carolina-born presidents: Andrew Jackson, James Polk, and Andrew Johnson. This is one of three molds made by sculptor Charles Keck for the original statue, which is at the state capitol. It was through the efforts of Sadie Patton, Mayor Al Edwards, and P. M. Camak that Hendersonville was able to obtain one of these molds. The statue can be seen at city hall.

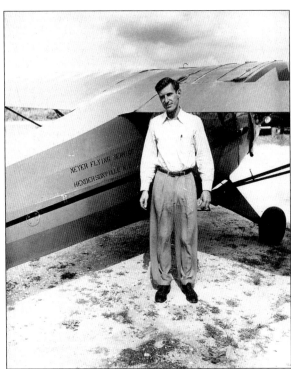

Shown here is Oscar Meyer. He started Meyer's Flying Service, which became Hendersonville Airport in about 1929. Oscar Meyer taught many young men to fly, including some who would become World War II pilots. He also taught Jack Edney, who would be air attaché to Ireland. (Courtesy of Charlie King.)

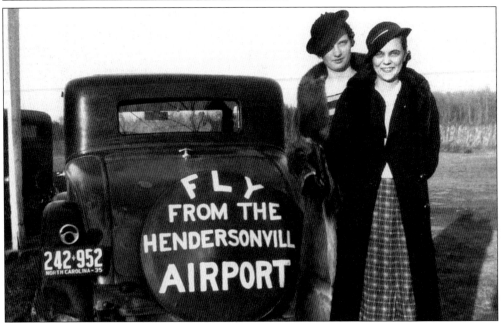

Pictured here are two young ladies dressed to "go to the airport." Just maybe they could catch a ride on a plane. The first commercial air service began c. 1937 when Eastern Airlines brought mail to the Asheville/Hendersonville airport, which is now an industrial park in Fletcher. The plane picked up mail that was "franked," honoring the history of flight. (Photograph courtesy of the Harry Thompson family; Baker-Barber Collection Community Foundation of Henderson County Courtesy.)

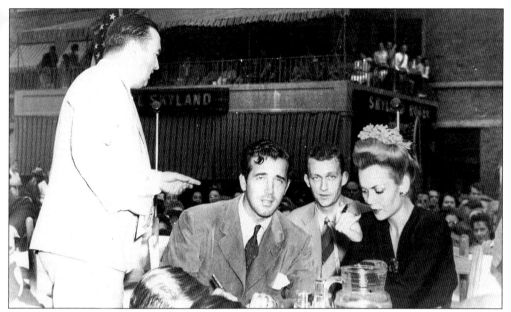

This is a photograph of a World War II war bond rally in about 1942. Shown from left to right are Harry E. Buchanan Sr., actor John Payne, Fred Reid (manager of the Carolina Theater), and actress Jane Wyman. Hendersonville was not on the travel list for John Payne and Jane Wyman, but Buchanan convinced them that the city would buy at least $1 million worth of bonds with their visit. They exceeded that amount. (Courtesy of the Buchanan family.)

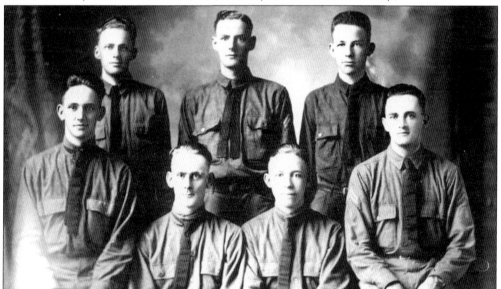

The Sixth Company formed *c.* 1911 in Hendersonville as part of the National Guard. When the United States declared war on Germany, the Sixth was sent to Fort Coswell outside of Wilmington, North Carolina. They were broken up into five other companies, most seeing duty overseas. From left to right are the following: (first row) Harry Williams, unidentified, R. L. Whitmire, and Fred Justice; (second row) unidentified, A. V. Edwards, and L. E. Lott. (Photograph courtesy of Charlie King; Baker-Barber Collection, Community Foundation of Henderson County.)

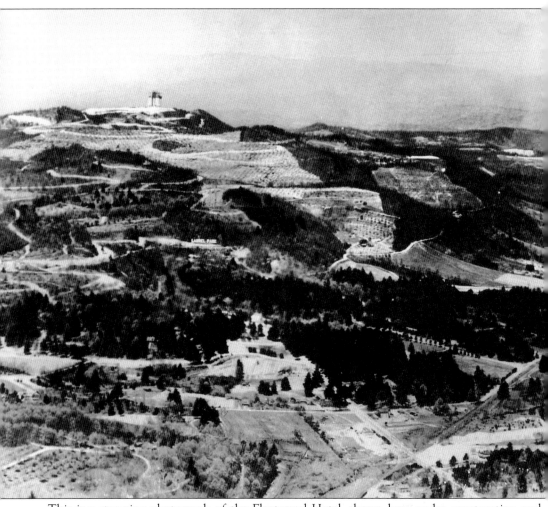

This is a stunning photograph of the Fleetwood Hotel, shown here under construction and surrounded by lush orchards and rolling terrain. During the Florida land-boom of the 1920s, Hendersonville was a destination for affluent Floridians. Laurel Park was promoted for having everything one could want—lakes for swimming, big-band entertainment, and a soon-to-be-finished luxurious hotel, the Fleetwood. Building began around 1925 on top of Echo Mountain. It was to be 14 stories (no 13th floor) with all the modern luxuries of the day. Then came the Great Depression, and everything was lost. Eventually the steel from the hotel was sold for scrap, and visitors could tour the grounds for 10 cents. (Photograph courtesy of Charlie King; Baker-Barber Collection, Community Foundation of Henderson County.)

Two
CHURCHES AND SCHOOLS

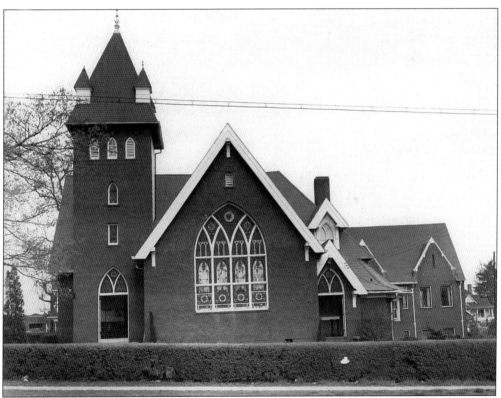

This photograph shows the second First Presbyterian Church building. It was constructed in 1905 on the corner of Seventh Avenue and Grove Street. The congregation was organized in 1852, and their first permanent building was built in 1859. The Sunday school building was a gift to the church from Capt. Ellison Adger Smyth as a memorial to his son. (Photograph courtesy of Mary Elizabeth Blair McLeod and First Presbyterian Church; Baker-Barber Collection, Community Foundation of Henderson County.)

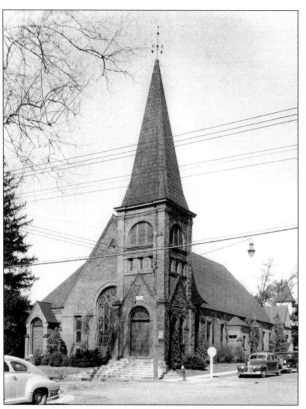

Shown here is the second building to house the First Baptist Church of Hendersonville. Built around 1889 and then rebuilt in 1911 and 1932; it was used until about 1954. The church was organized c. 1844 with 14 members. The congregation first met in their church building on Caswell and King Streets in the early 1850s. It is the oldest church within the city of Hendersonville. (Courtesy of First Baptist Church of Hendersonville.)

The photograph below shows the First Baptist Church Cherub Choir c. 1953. Some of the children appearing in this image are Larry Clouse and his cousin Judy Clouse, Susan Skaggs, Theresa Crouch, Kathie Loveland, and Pat Hutchinson. (Courtesy of Judy Clouse Loveland.)

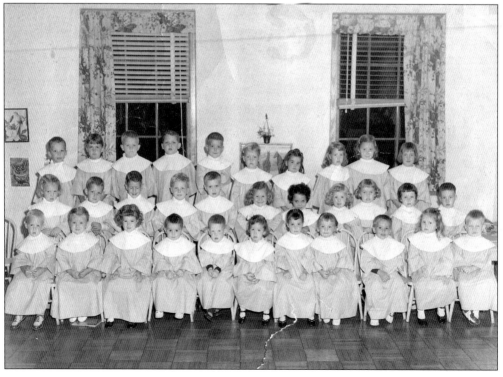

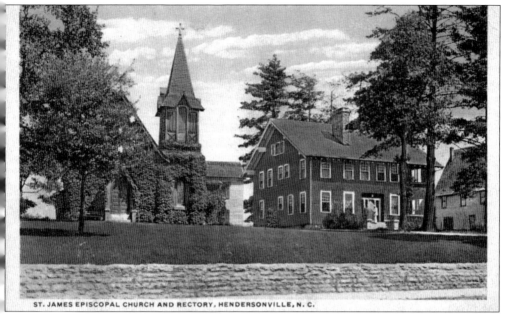

ST. JAMES EPISCOPAL CHURCH AND RECTORY, HENDERSONVILLE, N. C.

This c. 1900 postcard shows St. James Episcopal Church and its rectory on North Main Street, between Seventh and Eighth Avenues. The church bell, cast in Britain, was stolen during Stoneman's Raid through Hendersonville in 1865. The bell was replaced after the church rebuilt its congregation after the war. When Judson College was torn down, some of the stone was used in construction of the St. James sanctuary addition.

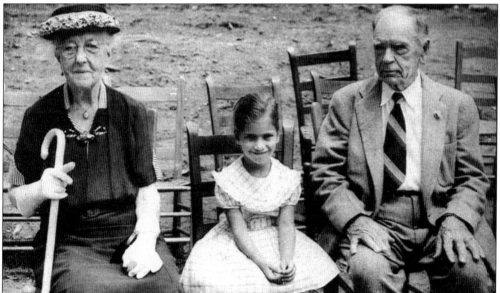

Appearing on the left is Lila Ripley Barnwell with an unidentified child and gentleman. Barnwell was born April 18, 1863 as the daughter of Col. Valentine Ripley who operated the first hotel and stagecoach line before the railroad arrived. Lila was a lifetime member of First Presbyterian Church, an authority on birds, and an accomplished poet. She died shortly before her 99th birthday and wrote her last poem, "Oklawaha," at age 95. (Courtesy of Mary Elizabeth Blair McLeod and First Presbyterian Church.)

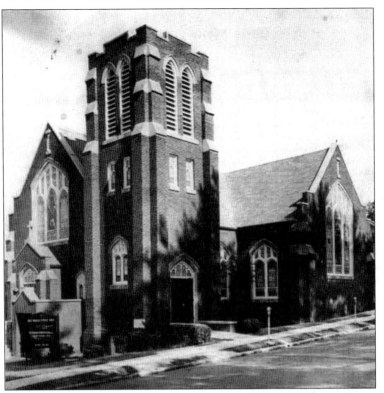

Starting in 1914, the Lutheran church began investigating prospects for a mission here. Visiting clergy preached in the courthouse during the winters of 1914–1915. Property on the corner of Seventh Avenue West and Church Street was purchased in 1921, and the cornerstone of Grace Lutheran Church was laid around 1924. The church is now located at Highway 64 West and Blythe Streets. (Courtesy of Bert Sitton, historian at Grace Lutheran Church.)

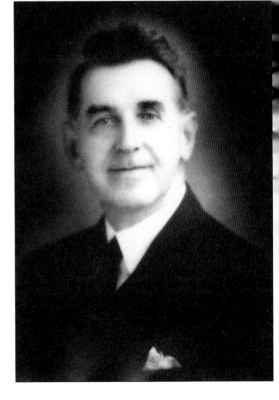

Rev. John David Mauney was the first permanent pastor to serve the Grace Lutheran congregation. He and his family, which included seven children, moved to Hendersonville around 1921 on a salary of $1,000 a year. Reverend Mauney brought his own small organ to church each Sunday until the congregation received a gift of a piano. He was also president of Hendersonville Ice Cream Makers. (Courtesy of Beverly Stone.)

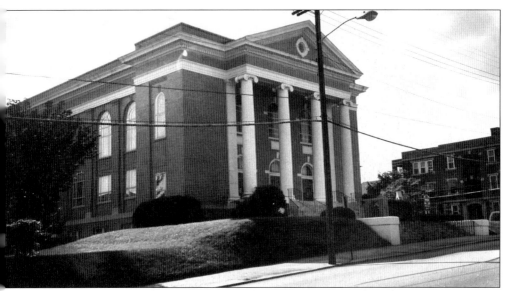

Shown here in a recent photograph is the church now known as First United Methodist Church. It has gone through several building changes and several name changes, including Hendersonville Methodist Episcopal Church and Hendersonville Methodist Episcopal Church South. In the original church, men sat on one side of the aisle and women on the other. The present sanctuary, designed by Erle Stillwell, was completed c. 1925 on one of the higher hills in downtown Hendersonville.

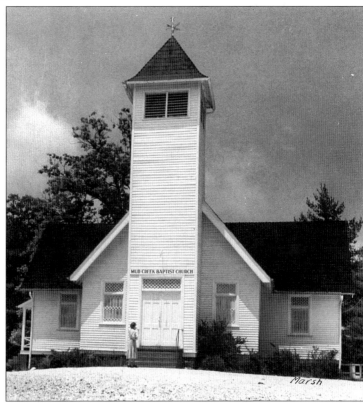

Mud Creek Baptist Church was organized as Mud Creek Meeting House c. 1804. The original congregation occupied a log building on land by the old Buncombe Turnpike belonging to Abraham Kuykendall. The original building was dismantled c. 1845, and a new structure was built. The building shown here was erected around 1900 with the help of the Norton sisters who owned Chanteloup Estate. Abraham Kuykendall and Charles Baring donated land. (Photograph by ? Marsh and courtesy of Charles Kuykendall.)

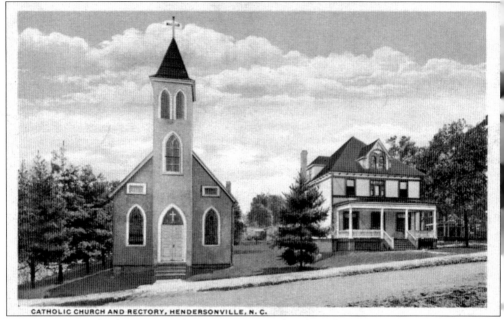

Shown here are the first Immaculate Conception Church and rectory, built c. 1912 as a seed church of St. Lawrence in Asheville. The dedicated but few Catholics struggled to survive with collections that ranged from $2.50 in the winter months to $25 in summer, thanks mostly to visitors from Florida and Charleston. (Courtesy of Immaculate Conception Church.)

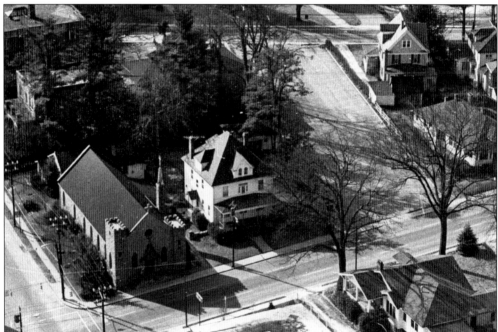

This c. 1950 aerial photograph shows the 1936 stone building that replaced the original Immaculate Conception Church. The house to the right of the church in this photograph is the rectory that housed the church's priests into the 1960s. The rectory also served as the first home of the Immaculata School from around 1926 to 1928. (Courtesy of Immaculate Conception Church.)

This photograph shows the original St. James Episcopal Church, which began as a mission of St. John in the Wilderness. Rev. Thomas S. W. Mott would conduct morning services at St. John's and afternoon services at St. James. In 1861, the first church building was consecrated. The Civil War imposed such hardships the church was dissolved around 1866. By 1894, the church ceased to be a mission and became an independent parish. The present church is an Erle Stilwell design. (Courtesy of St. James Episcopal Church.)

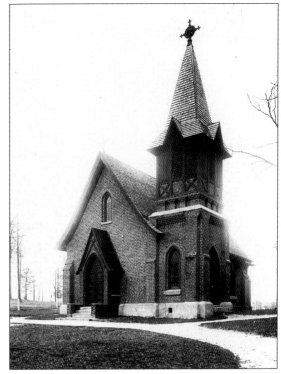

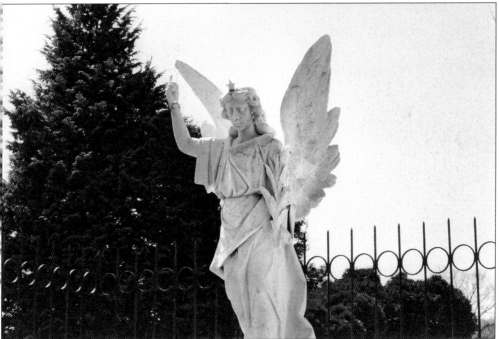

Keeping watch over the south side of Oakdale Cemetery is the angel monument referenced in Asheville author Thomas Wolfe's novel *Look Homeward Angel*. Crafted in Italian marble, the statue was purchased by Rev. H. F. Johnson and family from Thomas Wolfe's father, O. W. Wolfe. It is a prominent feature in the cemetery and part of the Johnson family plot.

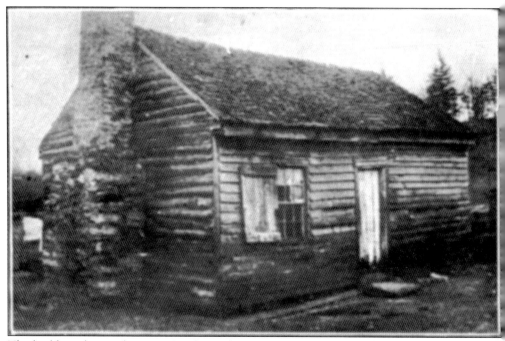

The building shown above on South Washington Street, along with the Old Judson College, housed the first students of the Hendersonville city school system, chartered by the State of North Carolina in 1901. (Courtesy of Hendersonville High School Alumni Association.)

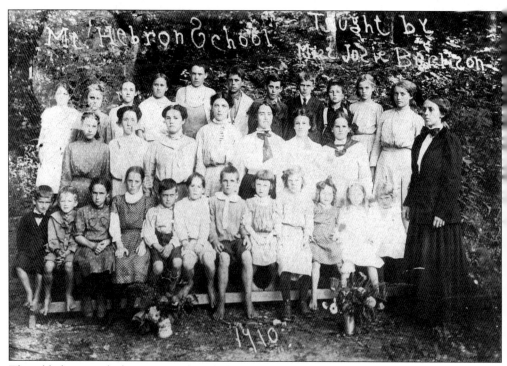

This old photograph shows an unidentified group of students at the Mt. Hebron School c. 1910. The teacher is Miss. Josie Burlison. (Courtesy of Deborah Summey.)

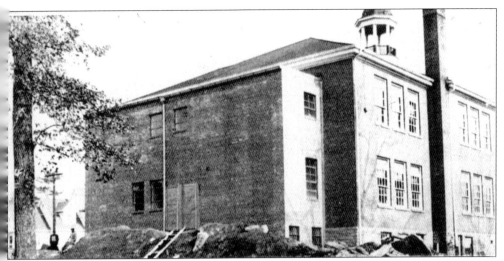

This photograph shows Hendersonville's first "modern" school under construction. It was built on land designated for educational purposes by the King land grant. Dedicated on March 15, 1912, the building accommodated 300 students in grades 1 through 11, employed 10 teachers, and began with a four-month session. Originally called the Fourth Avenue School, the name was changed to the Rosa Edwards School after the principal, Rosa Edwards, died. (Courtesy of Hendersonville High School Alumni Association.)

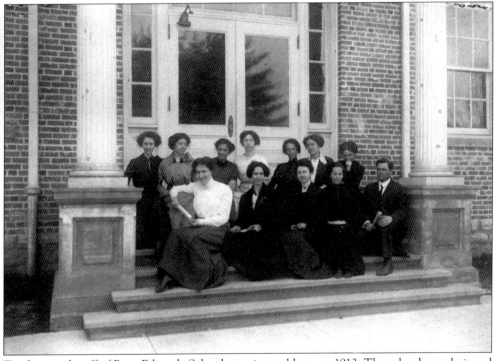

Teachers and staff of Rosa Edwards School are pictured here, c. 1913. The school was designed by Hendersonville architect Erle Stillwell. (Photograph courtesy of Charlie King; Baker-Barber Collection, Community Foundation of Henderson County.)

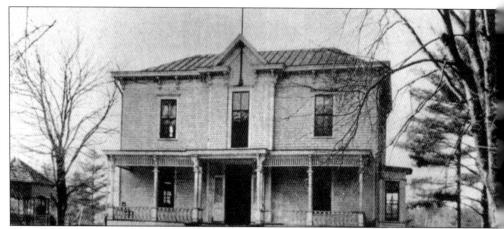

As enrollment at Rosa Edwards School neared 800 students c. 1919, high-school students were moved to the Anderson-Noterman House, shown here. Built by Maj. James Anderson, the house stood on a hill near the intersection of North Main and Church Streets, locally known as "Five Points." After his death in 1894, Anderson's heirs sold the property to the Noterman family. The property was later developed into Boyd Park. (Photograph courtesy of Hendersonville High School Alumni Association; Baker-Barber Collection, Community Foundation of Henderson County.)

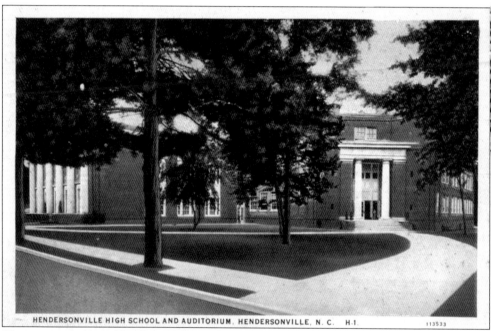

This postcard shows Hendersonville High School. The program for the school's dedication on December 3, 1926, read "[Hendersonville High School] Invites You to be Present at the dedication of the New Hendersonville Junior-Senior High School." Designed by Erle Stillwell, the building cost $320,000. Depending on where students lived in Hendersonville, they attended either Hendersonville High School or Rosa Edwards School for grades 1 through 11. (Courtesy of Jeff Miller.)

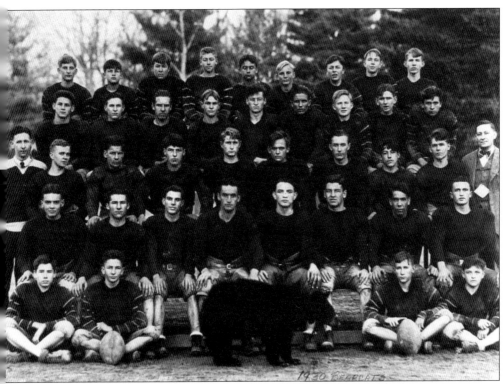

Pictured here is the 1930 Hendersonville High School "Bearcats." Pictured from left to right are the following: (first row) R. Todd, O. Brownlee, bear mascot, T. Loflin, and J. Sherrill; (second row) E. Waldrop, K. Arnette, D. Hill, H. Justus, T. McCarson, P. Greer, J. Todd, and C. Elliott; (third row) C. Murphy, P. Flanagan, E. Thompson, M. Bond, H. Brady, G. Zigraf, C. Coffey, W. Miller, E. Yelton, and "Pop" L. K. Singley (coach and principal); (fourth row) E. White, R. Orr, R. Cantrell, B. Wilkins, G. Tidd, R. Skipper, G. T. Orr, P. Byrd, and W. Bennett; (fifth row) B. Arledge, N. Miller, H. Williams, J. Tillitson, M. Johnson, H. Quarles, C. M. Pace, J. Morris, and A. Brown. (Courtesy of Hendersonville High School Alumni Association.)

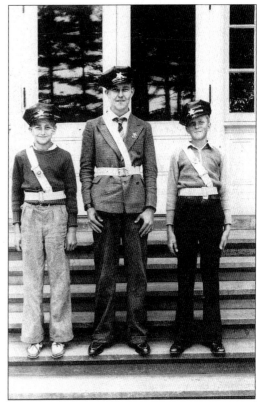

This picture shows the crossing guards for Rosa Edwards School, c. 1937. The school is currently used by the Henderson County Board of Education. The young man standing on the right is Raymond Edward Clouse. (Courtesy of Judy Clouse Loveland.)

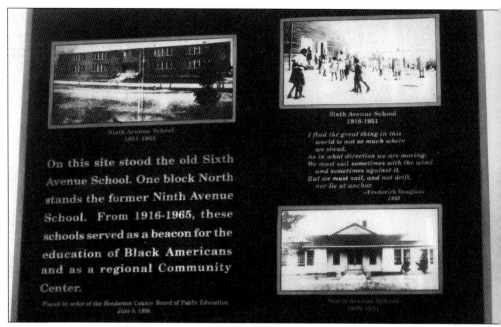

The Sixth Avenue School, and later the Ninth Avenue School, educated African American students of Henderson, Polk, and Transylvania counties. Ninth Avenue's class of 1965 was the last to graduate from the school after integration. The Sixth Avenue School was torn down in 1982, but the Ninth Avenue School remains part of Hendersonville Middle School. This photograph is of a marker located on Highway 64 West that shows pictures and a history of these two schools.

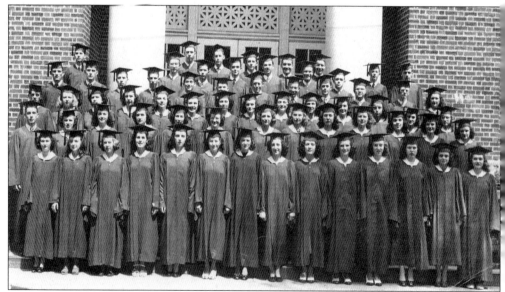

Pictured here is the Hendersonville High School class of 1948 at graduation. Space constraints preclude all identifications, but those appearing in the first row include from left to right Peggy Jones, Nancy Edney, B. J. Brock, Jean Rotha, Jean Burrell, Mary Frances Lyda, Kathleen Pack, Ester Prince, Betty Anders, Nancy Israel, Norma King, Anne Pack, Mary Ann Davis, and Carolyn Eye. (Photograph by Horace Mann and courtesy of Ellen Hutchinson Drake.)

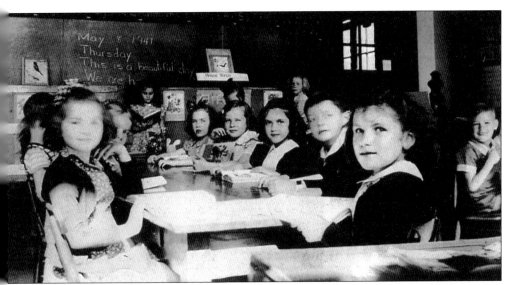

Miss Edna Scronce's first-grade class at Hendersonville High School poses on May 8, 1941, for this photograph. Beginning from the left is Jean Pace (reading), Pat Pullin, Mary Louise Shytle, Marguerite Briggs, T. Lee Osborne, and Jo Ann Stepp. (Courtesy of Jo Ann Stepp Fain.)

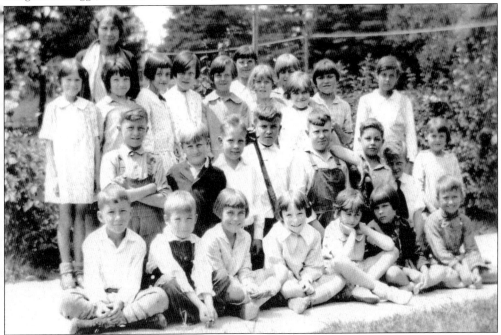

This photograph shows the first class to attend all 11 school years at Hendersonville High School (HHS). According to Dan Barber, his graduating class of 1964 was the last class to attend all years at HHS. The 12th grade was added in 1942. Pictured from left to right are the following: (first row) R. Bennett, P. Dermid, D. Ingram, R. Byers, A. Garren, two unidentified students; (second row) F. Turbeville, B. Lampley, E. Brown, B. Turner, unidentified, C. Truex, B. Shipman, unidentified; (third row) unidentified, S. Spears, F. Mitchell, K. Keith, M. Keith, unidentified, M. Skipper, two unidentified students, A. Dill, and O. Justice. The teacher is Seretha Sossaman. (Courtesy of Dr. William Lampley.)

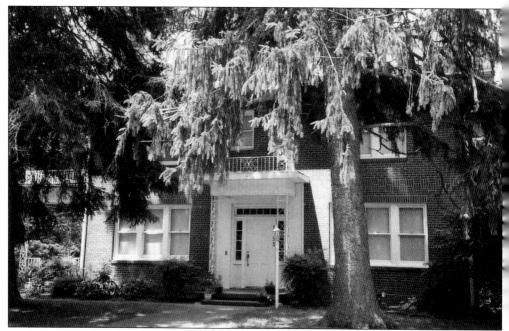

In 1927, Immaculate Conception Church purchased the Keith Property, a large brick house at 1133 Oakland Street (shown here in a recent photograph) to house Immaculata School. Classes met here for 22 years. The nuns and students who boarded at the school lived on the second floor.

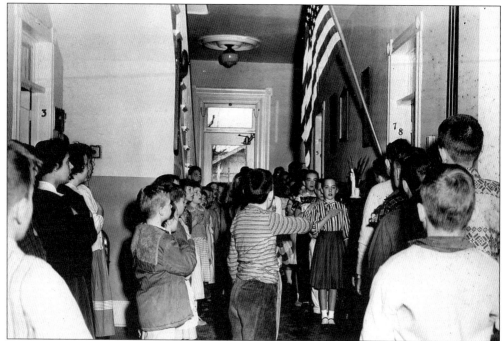

In 1949, Immaculata, with an enrollment of 125, moved to the Allworden Estate on the corner of Sixth Avenue and Buncombe Street. This photograph shows students saying the Pledge of Allegiance. Note the grade numbers on the door frames. (Courtesy of Immaculata Catholic School.)

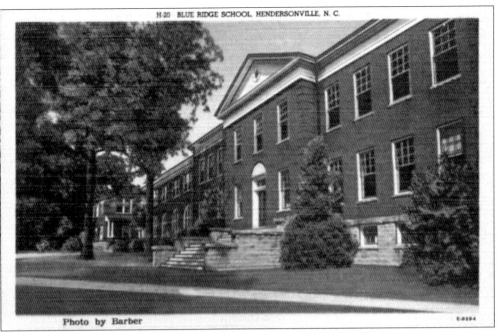

This postcard shows Blue Ridge School for Boys with the headmaster's home in the distance. Founded in 1913 by Joseph Randolph Sandifer, it grew rapidly attracting students from 40 states and 15 foreign countries. Local boys could attend as day students. Professor Sandifer passed away in 1956. Mrs. Sandifer continued to operate the school until around 1968. The school was located where the Blue Ridge Mall is now located.

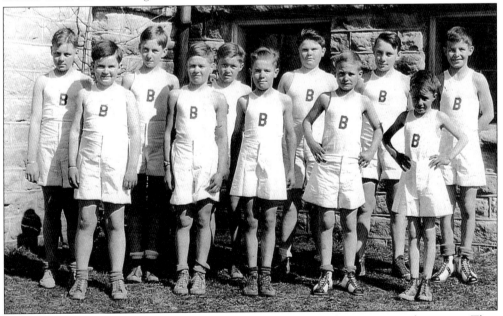

Shown here are students from the Blue Ridge School for Boys during an outside activity. They appear to be one of the lower grades, as the school educated boys aged 10 and up. Class size was usually about 10 boys. Three nieces of Professor Sandifer were the only girls to attend and graduate from the school. (Courtesy of the Harry Thompson family.)

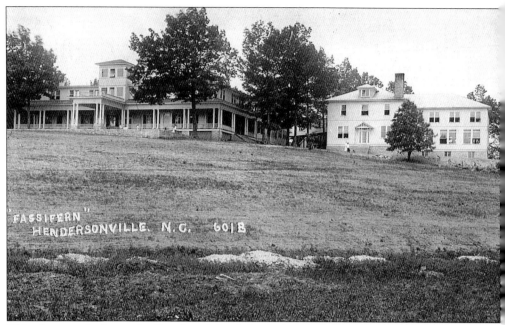

This photograph shows the Fassifern School for Girls, which operated until 1962. Started in Lincolnton, the school was brought to Hendersonville by Kate Shipp and her sister. It was located on Fleming Street and Asheville Highway in 1914. The school accommodated all grades, and most students were boarders, though some local girls did attend as day students. In 1925, the school was sold to Rev. Joseph L. Sevier. (Courtesy of Hendersonville Chamber of Commerce.)

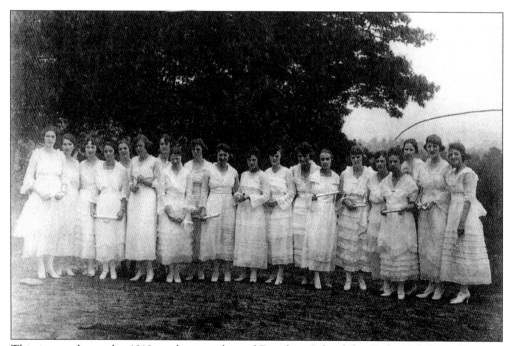

This image shows the 1919 graduating class of Fassifern School for Girls. Halide Williams of Killarney, is the fifth girl from the right. (Courtesy of Carolyn Smith Lockaby.)

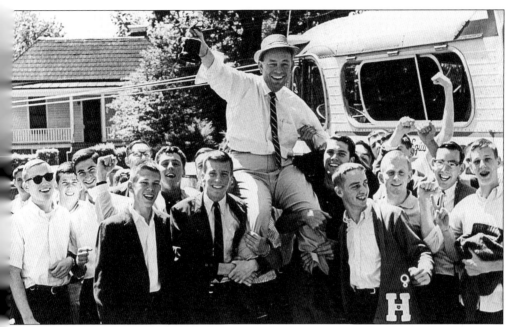

The jubilant 1964 HHS track team is pictured after winning the North Carolina state championship. Members of this team were also on the 1963–1964 state-championship-winning cross country team; 1963 was the first year the cross-country competed on the state level in North Carolina. These championships were prior to the sorting of schools into different divisions. From left to right are M. Harper, G. Carswell, D. Kaplan, T. Cosgrove, R. Miller, E. Allen, Coach Rob Brown, D. Drake, B. Crawford, D. Starnes, C. Hunter, and G. Barber. Dan Barber's arm can be seen behind his brother. (Courtesy of Dan Barber.)

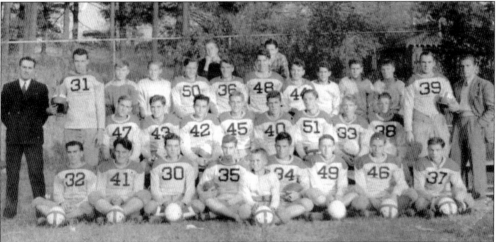

Pictured here is the Hendersonville High School football team from c. 1938. On the left is Coach Langerburg and on the right is Coach Carter. Pictured from left to right are the following: (first row) L. A. Crouch, B. Staton, F. Hawkins, R. Steidez, unidentified boy, J. Chandler, P. Pace, Sifty Griffin, H. Smith; (second row) Horse Sparks, C. Drake, Daisy Mae O'Brien, B. Lyday, B. Johnson, C. McCorkle, M. Spears, Flash Johnson, Sub McManaway, Handsome Anders; (third row) K. Boyd, B. Weston, J. Cole, R. Nanney, Shine Patterson, Stoogie Lenard, B. Gesser, H. Hill, M. Bowman, and two unidentified men in the rear. (Courtesy of the Charley Drake family.)

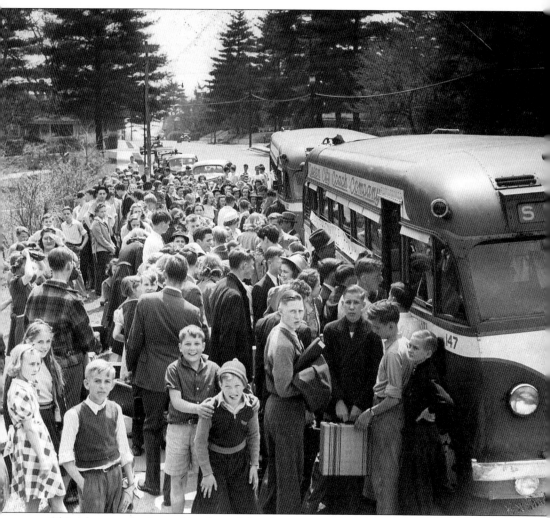

This photograph shows friends and family meeting the Hendersonville High School band buses as they returned from a state competition. From the bottom left-hand corner going right are Annie Sue French, Sally Myer, Cliff Collins, Jimmy Williams, Gordon Williams, and Earl Dolbee (holding a suitcase). (Photograph courtesy of Annie Sue Foster; Baker-Barber Collection, Community Foundation of Henderson County.)

Three

HOUSES AND HISTORIC DISTRICTS

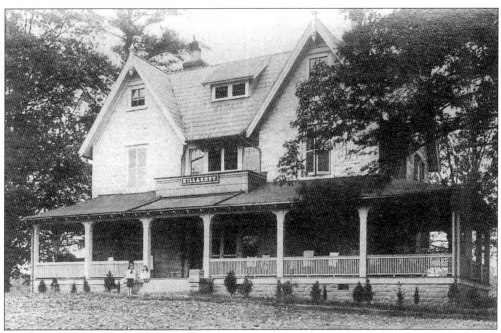

Killarney was built by William Bryson of South Carolina c. 1858. Purchased around 1895 by Annie E. Patton, the Killarney property would become Hyman Heights Historic District. In 1908, while owned by William H. Rhett, a third story and wrap-around porches were added to the building. These changes and additions were designed by Richard Sharp Smith, designer of the Henderson County courthouse and supervising architect of the Biltmore House in Asheville, North Carolina. (Courtesy of E. Mark Fender.)

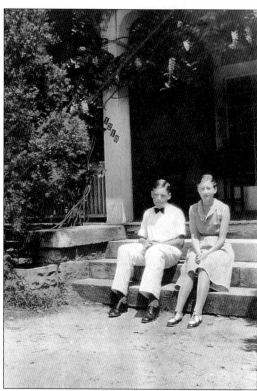

Photographed on the front steps of Killarney, their grandmother's home, cousins Bob Henry and Carolyn Smith are photographed c. 1931. This photograph shows Killarney after the Richard Sharp Smith renovation of 1908. Killarney is now a bed and breakfast. (Courtesy of Carolyn Smith Lockaby.)

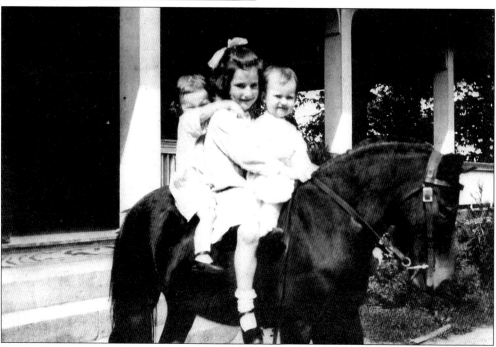

This c. 1913 photograph shows from left to right Carolyn Smith, Elizabeth Williams, and a friend taking a ride on Carolyn's pony, Prince. The Killarney porch is in the background. (Courtesy of Carolyn Smith Lockaby.)

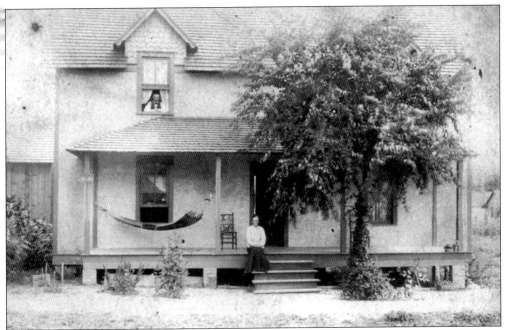

This c. 1910 photograph of a house on Allen Street. The house was located behind the present ABC store. The owners are shown catching a cool breeze. (Courtesy of David W. Cooley.)

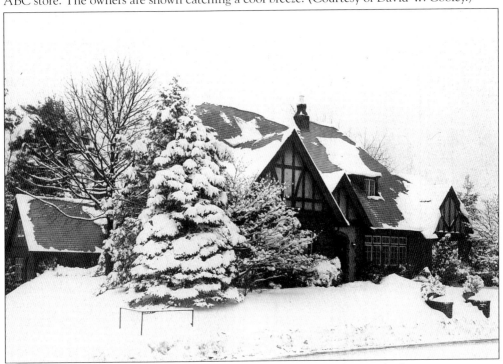

Shown here in a c. 1948 photograph is the home of Dr. Drafts, a doctor who began practicing in Hendersonville as early as 1905. This home was on the southeast corner of Church Street and Sixth Avenue West across from the Methodist Church steps. (Photograph courtesy of Charlie King; Baker-Barber Collection, Community Foundation of Henderson County.)

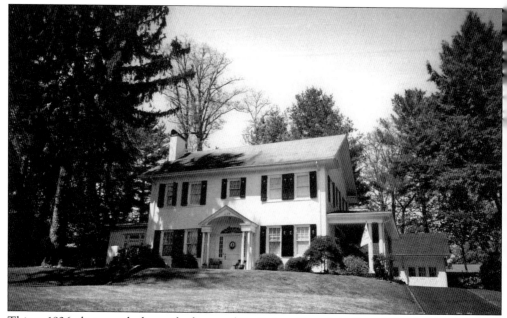

This c. 1926 photograph shows the home of Dr. Robert Sample built at 1125 Highland Avenue in Hyman Heights, located across Waynesville Street from Patton Memorial Hospital where he practiced. Hyman Heights, now a local and nationally registered historic district, began when William A. Garland developed approximately 25 acres that he purchased in 1905 from Annie Eliza Patton of Killarney House. At one time, the Pattons owned over 1,100 acres in this area.

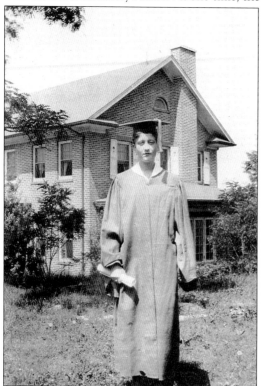

This photograph shows Carolyn Smith on the day of her high school graduation in 1931. She is standing in the side yard of Killarney. Dr. Sample's house is seen in the background at 1125 Highland Avenue. Dr. Sample's home was originally red brick then repainted white by the second owners, Dr. and Mrs. Jim Lutz. The third owners, Dr. and Mrs. David Glenn, expanded the back part of the house for more living space. (Courtesy of Carolyn Smith Lockaby.)

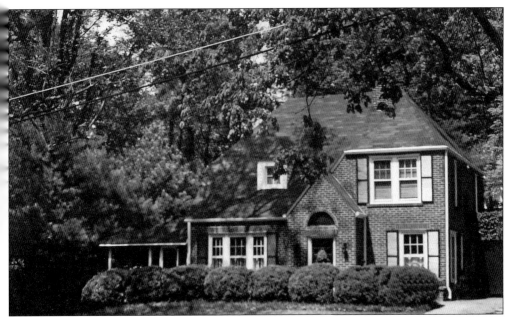

Shown here is a house built in the Norman cottage style at 1324 Highland Avenue, erected c. 1925. This part of Highland Avenue, along with Regal and Ridgecrest Streets, was platted in July 1923 as part of the Mount Royal subdivision. The *Times-News* noted in 1923 that large "villa" sites were for sale from $585 to $985, and deed restrictions indicated that "no person shall be allowed to erect unsightly and inartistic dwellings."

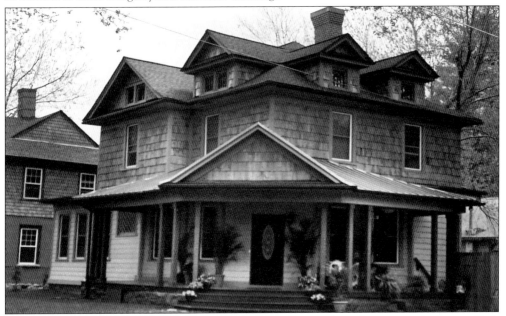

The house at 826 Dale Street shows one of the few Queen Anne houses in the Lenox Park Historic District. It appears on the original 1908 plat for Columbia Park. Albert and Ethel Beck, of Beck Hardware Company, lived in this house from 1926 to 1951. The house was known as Beck House or Beck Villa, a boarding house for summer tourists. A brochure from 1931 noted a single room with meals, per week, cost $12.50 to $15.

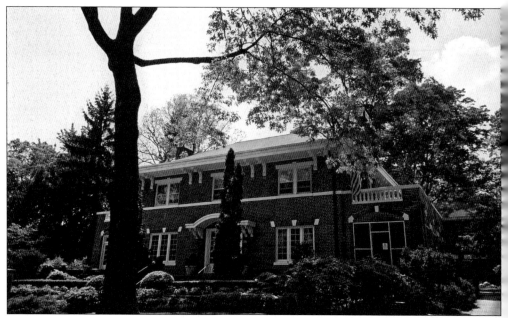

Shown in this photograph is an Italian Renaissance-Revival house built c. 1926 by contractor John Forest for his residence. It overlooked the park laid out in the Druid Hills neighborhood. The *Times-News* advertised the neighborhood as having "over a mile of paved streets, over a mile of sewers, over a mile of water mains, ornamental entrances, parks, tennis courts for exclusive use of residents, lights and telephones."

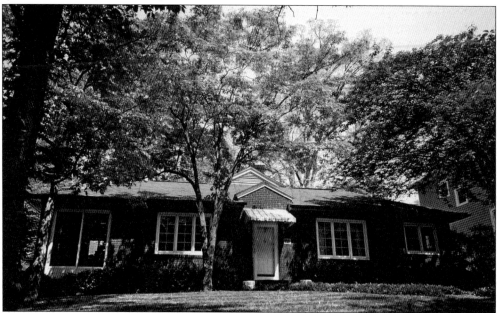

Records show that Virginia Byrd purchased 1642 Kensington Road on October 27, 1925. During the heyday of Hendersonville's summer tourist season, the Byrd family rented the home and moved into a less-expensive rental property. This allowed the mortgage to be paid in four years. When the house was purchased from the Byrd family in July 1983, everything inside and out, except for the brick, had been painted yellow.

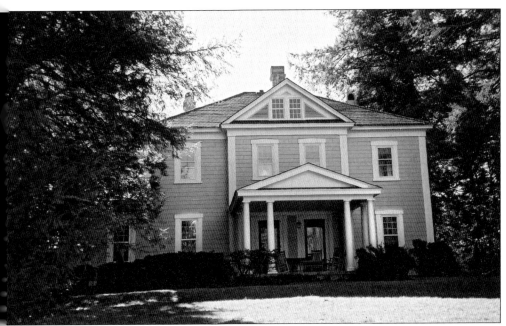

Frederick Rutledge began the estate known as Brooklands in 1828. The house he built is now encompassed within the guesthouse, shown below. Charles and Mary Edmondston of Charleston built the main house, shown above, and outbuildings. In 1841, Brooklands was purchased by the British consul to Charleston, Edmund Molyneaux. Abandoned during the Civil War, Theodore and Louise Barker purchased it around 1881. It was one of the largest estates in the area. In 1917, Brooklands was bought by Henry Ficken, a descendent of Revolutionary War general William Moultrie. It is currently the private home of Mr. and Mrs. C. E. Staton. (Courtesy of Mr. and Mrs. C. E. Staton.)

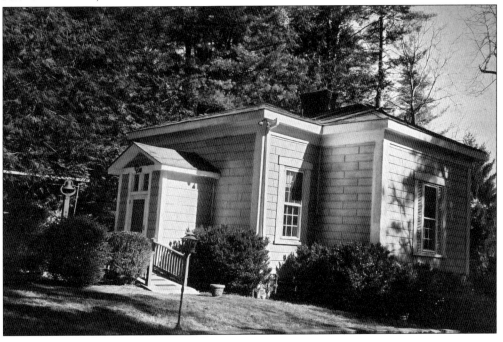

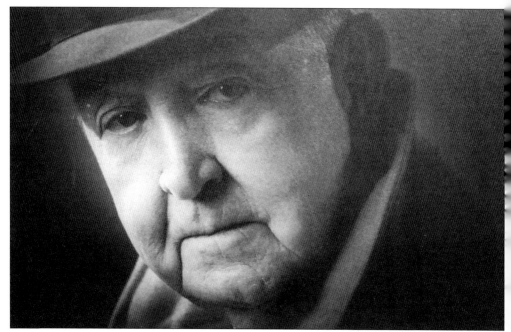

Erle Gulick Stillwell was born in Hannibal, Missouri, on August 29, 1885. He attended the United States Naval Academy in Annapolis, Maryland, and studied at the University of North Carolina, Cornell University, and University of Pennsylvania. In 1907, he married the daughter of William A. Smith, developer of Laurel Park. In 1916, Stillwell opened an architecture practice and later became a founding partner in the Asheville-based firm Six Associates. Erle Stillwell died on October 22, 1978. (Courtesy of St. James Episcopal Church.)

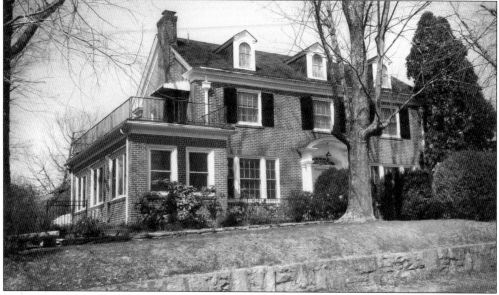

Situated on the corner of Fourth Avenue West and Ehringhaus Street is another home designed by Erle Stillwell. It was built c. 1925 by James P. Grey Jr., whose father started the Grey Hosiery Mill. After his father moved on to Bristol, Tennessee to open another mill, James Grey Jr. and his uncle, Charles Grey, stayed and ran the mill until its sale in 1965.

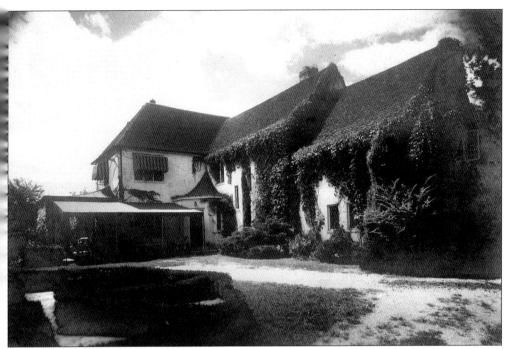

This c. 1940 photograph shows the home Erle Stillwell built for himself at 1300 Pinecrest Drive. The brick home was completed in 1926. The living room has cherry paneling, a rough plaster ceiling, and a limestone fireplace. Throughout the house is oak flooring, call buttons for domestic help, and cedar-lined closets. This home is designated as a local historic landmark by the City of Hendersonville. (Courtesy of Miller Medina.)

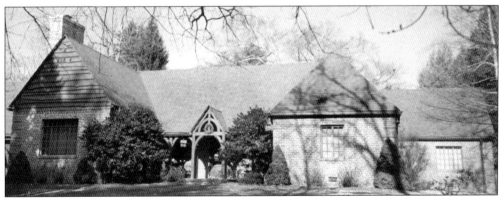

After losing the residence at 1300 Pinecrest Drive in the Depression, Erle Stillwell designed, built, and lived at 541 Blythe Street from its completion in 1935 until his death in 1978. Located across the backyard from his first home, it exhibits the same high degree of craftsmanship and features of his first home. This home is a local historic landmark, as designated by the City of Hendersonville. (Courtesy of Mr. and Mrs. Michael Blanton.)

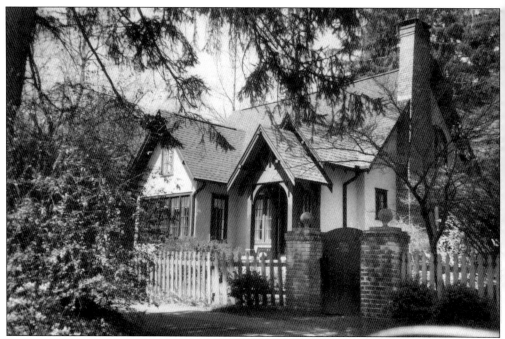

Built c. 1925 by O. E. Hedge, 525 Ehringhaus Street was owned for over 50 years by Margery Burrowes. In 1972, poet John Travers Moore and his wife, author Margaret Moore, rented the home, naming it Poethaven. Mr. Moore authored books of poetry, including *The Story of Silent Night* and the *Pepito* trilogy.

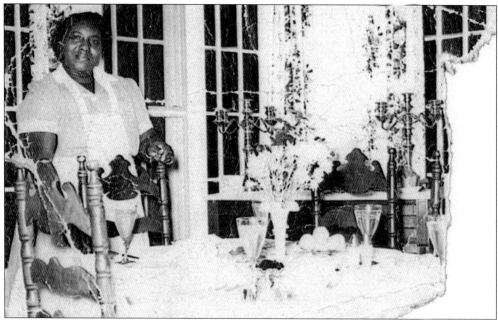

As shown in this early photograph of a beautifully set table and domestic help, entertaining was always important at 525 Ehringhaus Street. Legends written and illustrated by the Moores adorned the walls throughout the house. These paintings have been painted over, but a fixative was used to allow for future restoration. (Courtesy of Lisa Clark.)

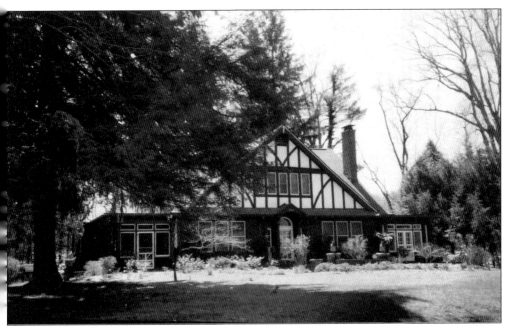

Shown here is a photograph of 1110 Fourth Avenue West, designed in 1925 by Erle Stillwell for the William M. Sherard family. William Sherard was mayor of Hendersonville from 1929 until 1932. This house, along with 243 other buildings, is now part of the West Side Historic District. Listed on the National Register in 2001, it is the largest historic district in Hendersonville.

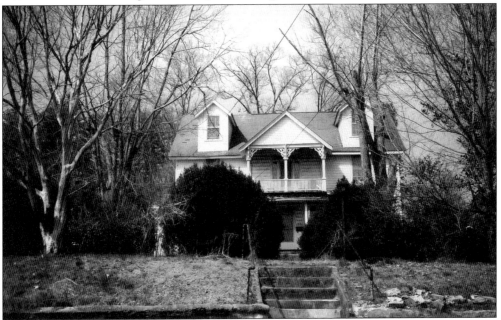

Shown here is the Columbus Mills Pace House at 813 Fifth Avenue West. Mr. Pace was born c. 1845 and served as the first Justice of the Peace in Henderson County, clerk of Superior Court, and county commissioner. He was a partner with W. A. Smith during the development of Laurel Park. As with many homes, Columbus Mills Pace House was used for boarding and known as Locust Lodge. The old smoke house is still visible from Fifth Avenue.

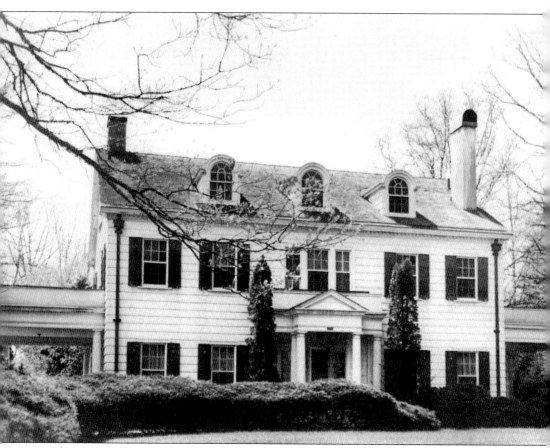

This c. 1940 photograph of 1230 Fifth Avenue West shows the house during the Buchanan era. The house was designed by Erle Stillwell and built by the Hobbs family c. 1920. Hit hard by the Depression, Mr. Hobbs sold the home to the Buchanan family, who lived there for over 30 years. Now owned and operated by Mehmet and Lale Ozelsel as Mélange Bed and Breakfast, the house is active with weddings and parties throughout the year. (Courtesy of Jean Buchanan.)

Four

HOTELS AND BOARDING HOUSES

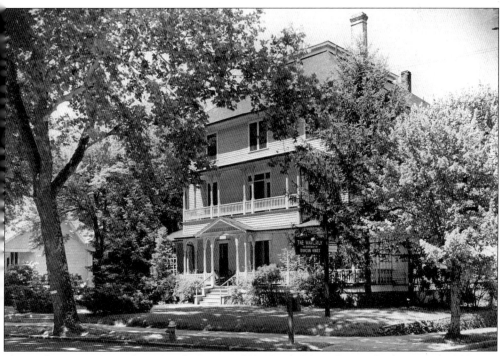

Shown here c. 1950 is the Waverly Inn on 783 North Main Street. Built around 1900 as a tourist lodge, the Waverly has stood the test of time and is one of the most pleasant inns in Hendersonville. The Waverly has hosted many of Hendersonville's well-known visitors who have all been delighted by the big broad porch and its comfortable rocking chairs. (Photograph courtesy of John and Diane Shirey; the Baker-Barber Collection Community, Foundation of Henderson County.)

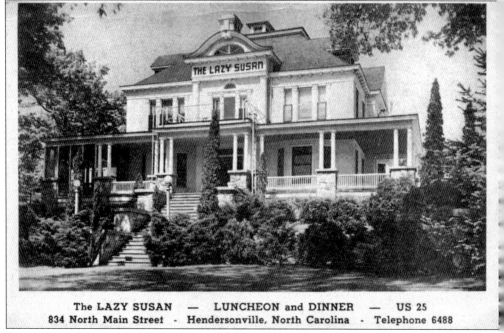

Pictured on this postcard is the beautiful Lazy Susan. Built as the Rhett House c. 1899, it stood near the present site of Bruce Drysdale School. The building operated as the Lazy Susan Restaurant, serving lunch and dinner, until 1941, when it became the Elks Lodge. The Elks used this house as their headquarters until they moved to the Park Hill Inn. The telephone number for the Lazy Susan was 6488.

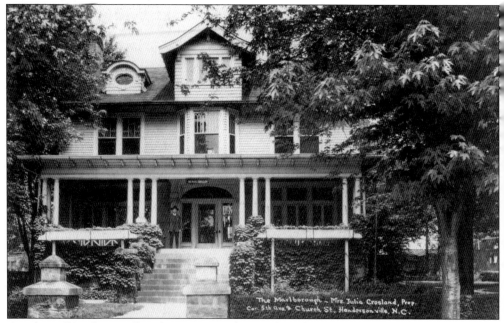

Another of Hendersonville's charming guesthouses from the past is pictured here. This building was known as the Marlborough Inn, located on the corner of Fifth Avenue West and Church Street. The proprietor at the time of this photograph was Julie Crosland.

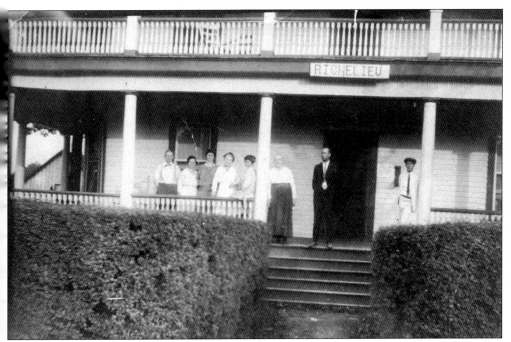

The Richelieu was located on Pace Street near the railroad station and served as a boarding house for many years. It was owned by Annie Stowers, whose daughter, Marjie, is pictured second from left with unidentified guests. This photograph was taken c. 1900. It is thought that Marjie met her future husband when he was a guest here. (Courtesy of Annie Sue Foster.)

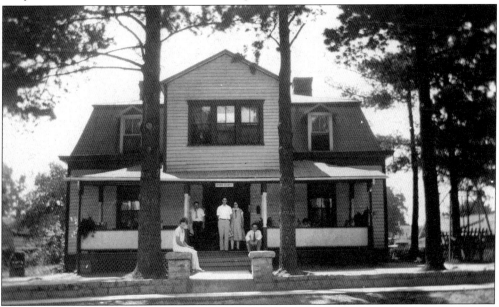

This is the Pine Hurst Lodge, located where the steps to the Henderson County Courthouse are today. Owned by Mrs. Glover T. Orr, who is pictured standing on the far right with unidentified guests, the Pine Hurst was known for its robust breakfasts and lunches, served family-style. There were great quantities of fresh home-cooked foods, and the cost was $1.50 per person. Everything was cooked on a wood stove. (Courtesy of Barbara Peace Lohman.)

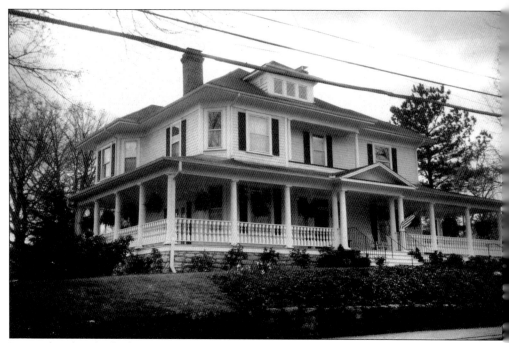

Pictured is the Elizabeth Lee Inn, built c. 1893 by the Roberts family. After Mr. Robert's death, the house, now in the West Side Historic District, was known as the Fifth Avenue Guesthouse. In the 1950s, Charles and Verona Rogers bought the property. Charles and his brother, Harry, owners of a hosiery mill, had a falling out about whether panty hose would become popular with ladies. The mill was subsequently closed. (Courtesy of Cindy and Michael Baer.)

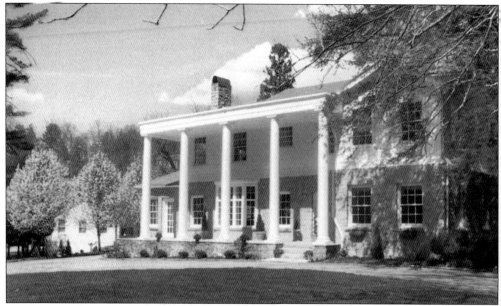

Seen here is Pinebrook Manor on Kanuga Road, built c. 1910 by the Wheeler family. It was built of rock quarried on the property. In 1945, it became the home of Jane and Ivor Pardee, who lived there for many years. The property has been lovingly restored by Melanie and Terry Welton, who operate a bed and breakfast. (Courtesy of Melanie and Terry Welton.)

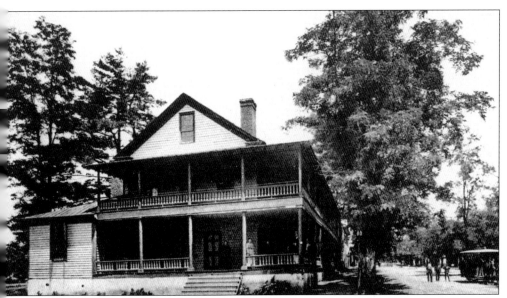

Photographed above is the Ripley House, Hendersonville's first hotel, built c. 1842 on the northwest corner of Main Street and Second Avenue. Built by Col. Valentine Ripley, it served as a stagecoach stop along the Buncombe Turnpike between Charleston and Asheville. The Ripley House was the center of social activity on Main Street from the time it opened and through its expansions. It ended as the St. John Hotel had a pebbledash exterior, 150 rooms, a grand ballroom, and was three stories high. After the summer season in October 1915, a fire of suspicious origin engulfed the building. People's National Bank acted as a firewall, preventing the fire from going farther. The site remained empty for about 20 years until an office building was erected, then Western Auto was built on the north side about 1961. (Photograph of original hotel courtesy of Charlie King; Baker-Barber Collection, Community Foundation of Henderson County.)

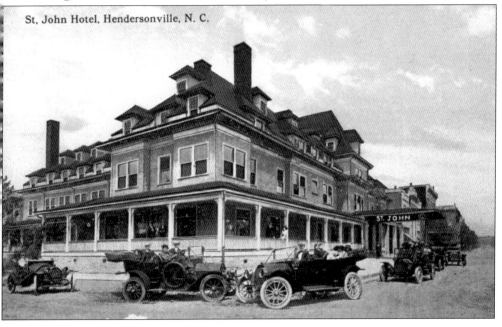

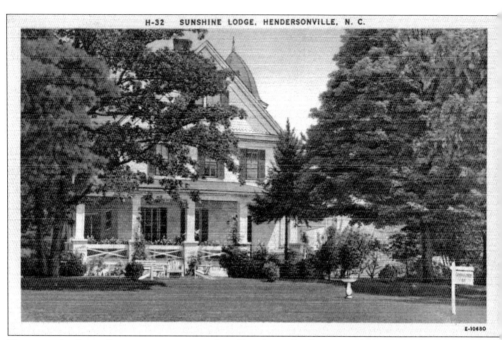

Photographed on this vintage postcard is Sunshine Lodge, c. 1920. Located at 613 Fourth Avenue West, it boasted of fine accommodations, excellent food, and a refined clientele, all located in "The Land of the Sky."

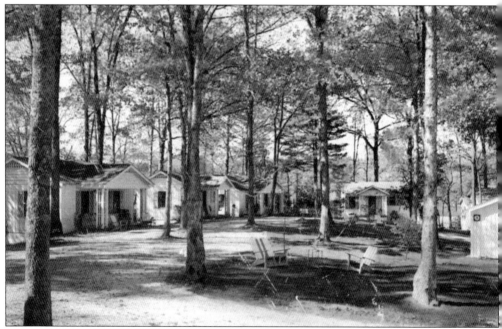

In addition to hotels and guesthouses, Hendersonville has long been known for its cottage colonies. Families from warmer climates came to Hendersonville for weeks, months, or the entire summer to enjoy fresh air and cool summer evenings. One of these cottage colonies, pictured here, is Mountain Aire Lodge. It offered a large swimming pool, tennis courts, and outdoor grills. (Courtesy of his honor, Mayor Fred Neihoff.)

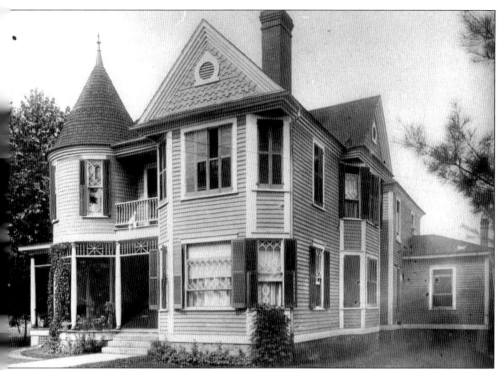

Here is a photograph of the Claddagh Bed and Breakfast when it was named the Charleston. It was the city's first bed and breakfast and is located at 755 North Main Street. It was built as a boarding house c. 1888 by W. A. Smith and called the Smith-Green House. Between 1912 and 1922, a third story was added, and after extensive renovations in 1985, the inn acquired its present name, the Claddagh. (Courtesy of Sinikka Bell.)

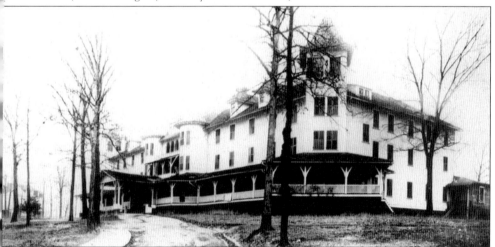

Pictured here is the Wheeler Hotel c. 1895. Located where Bruce Drysdale School is today, the hotel had 100 rooms and a livery stable on Locust Street. The dance pavilion, which burned in 1927 in a sad but spectacular fire, hosted bands such as Hal Kemp's orchestra. During a blizzard in 1930, the hotel itself burned. Snow-covered rooftops prevented many nearby houses from burning. (Photograph courtesy of John and Diane Shirey, Baker-Barber Collection, Community Foundation Henderson County.)

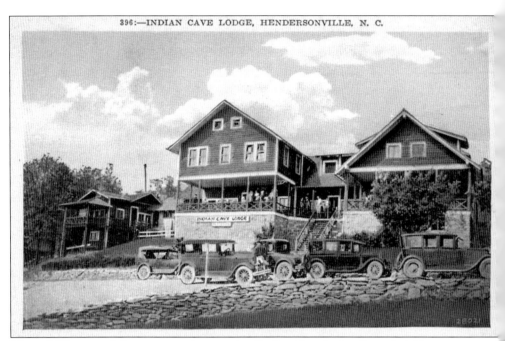

This c. 1920 postcard shows a great photograph of Indian Cave Lodge. Boxer Jack Dempsey trained in the outdoor boxing ring set up for him in front of the lodge. The mountain views are spectacular from this very special Laurel Park location. The lodge has been replaced by a private residence.

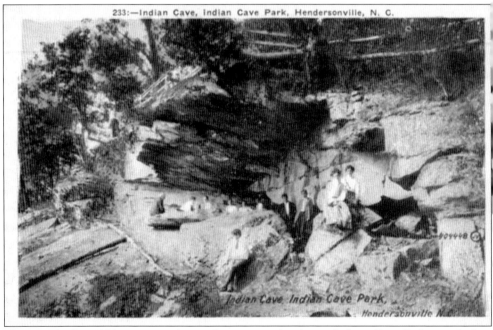

Photographed c. 1920, a group of picnickers enjoys the day at Indian Cave Park near Indian Cave Lodge. The park was a very special place for vacationers staying at the lodge. Picnics were packed and excursions were made for all-day outings.

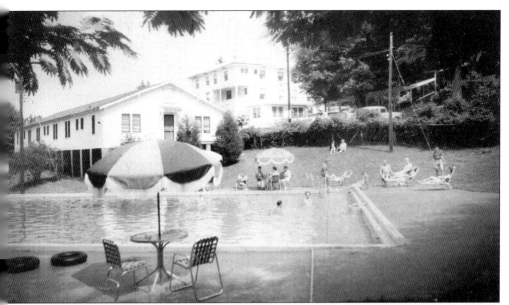

Pictured here is the Duncraggan Inn. Purchased from Roberta Morgan and ABC Sports's Roone Arledge in 1931, the Wise family ran the inn as a summer resort for over 30 years. Located at the end of Third Avenue West, the property then passed to a charitable organization that in turn sold it to Stuart Rubin and Partners in 1975. The inn has since burned. (Courtesy of Staci Blatt.)

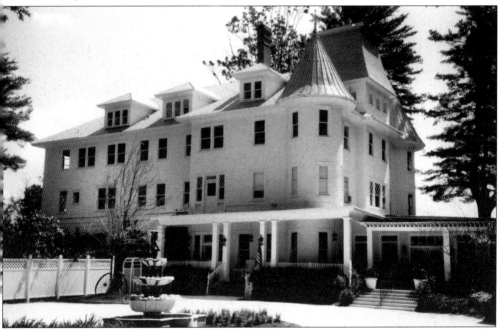

Here is a recent photograph of the Copper Crest Inn, the reincarnation of the Osceola Lake Inn, built around 1908. The Rubin family purchased the hotel and property c. 1940. It was a popular vacation spot for Floridians, offering entertainment, three meals a day, and sporting activities. The inn is once again thriving as the Copper Crest Inn. (Courtesy of Ed and Barbara Hernando.)

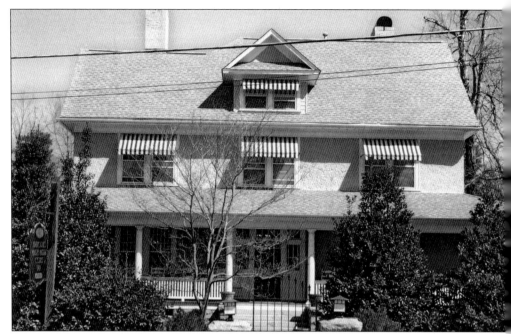

Here is a photograph of the Mary Mills Coxe House built in 1911 by the widow of Col. Franklin Coxe, an Asheville real estate developer. The house is believed to be one of the few remaining pebbledash houses in Henderson County. Mrs. Coxe died in 1914, and the house passed to the Wharton family who called it Gray Gables. The house is now an inn and is home to the Gables Restaurant. (Courtesy of Brenda and Bruce Tompkins.)

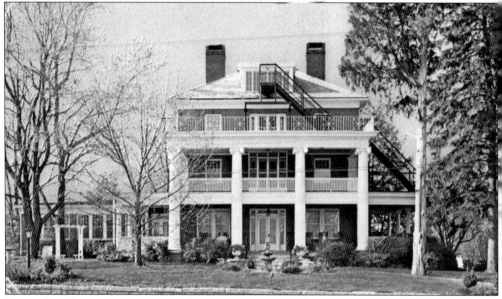

Pictured on this postcard is the Cedars, built in 1913 as a hotel by Jennie Bailey who purchased the property for $2,200. The price tells of the elevated property values due to the resort land-boom. It advertised, "no consumptives, open all year, hot water, heat/running hot and cold water in every room." It operated as a hotel until 1976 when it sold to Clifton Shipman. It now hosts special events. (Courtesy of Tommy Shipman.)

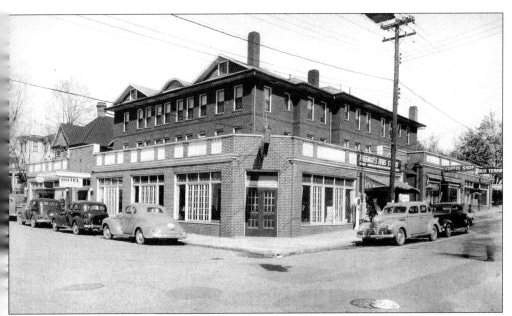

Seen here c. 1945 on the corner of Fourth Avenue West and Church Street, where the Dogwood Parking Lot is today, is the Hodgewell Hotel owned by W. B. Hodges, president of the State Trust Company. Visitors could arrive by bus, stop for breakfast, buy a newspaper at Freeman's, weigh themselves for a penny, get a haircut, and check in without crossing the street. WHKP had its first headquarters in this building. (Courtesy of David W. Cooley and Hendersonville Chamber of Commerce.)

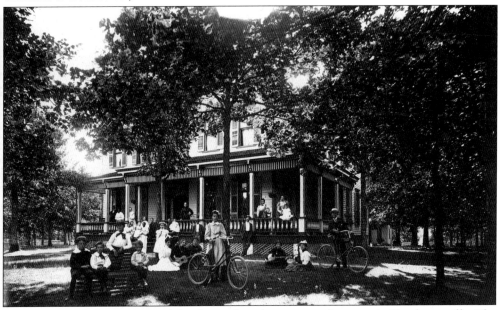

This photograph features several families gathered on a nice afternoon in Hendersonville. The structure appears to have been one of the many boarding houses that served families escaping the summer heat from warmer parts of the South. Many families would spend the entire summer season at a Hendersonville inn or boarding house. (Photograph courtesy of Charlie King; Baker-Barber Collection, Community Foundation of Henderson County.)

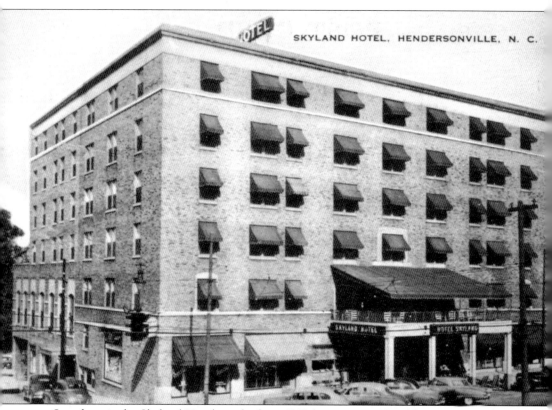

Seen here is the Skyland Hotel was built in 1928 by a group of local businessmen who wanted a "real hotel" on Main Street. It boasted a roof garden, ballroom (now the Skyland Movie Theatre), and an excellent restaurant. Many famous people have stayed at the hotel throughout the years, including Lee Marvin, Minnie Pearl, and F. Scott Fitzgerald. Fitzgerald stayed in rooms that are now part of the Arts Center.

Five
BUSINESS AND INDUSTRY

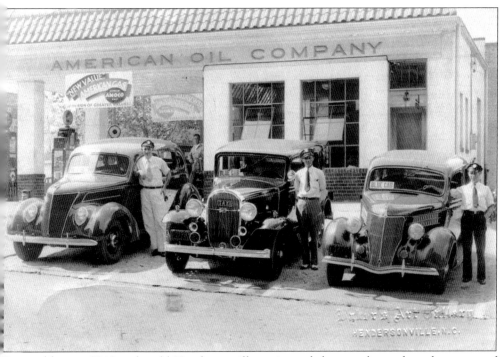

Pictured here c. 1940 is the old Hendersonville taxi stand that was located on the corner of Allen and Main Streets. Properly attired in shirt and tie are unidentified drivers, waiting for a fare. (Courtesy of Ron Miller, Baker-Barber Collection, Community Foundation of Henderson County.)

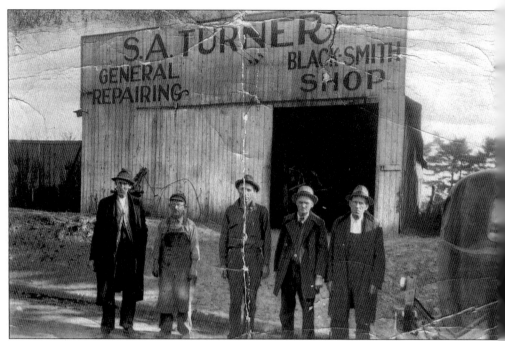

James Fanning Corn, second from left, is shown here at the S. A. Turner blacksmith shop in 1926, which was located on the corner of First Avenue and King Street. He worked at several blacksmith shops in the area, including the Biltmore Estate in Asheville from 1917 to 1918. (Courtesy of Jo Ann Stepp.)

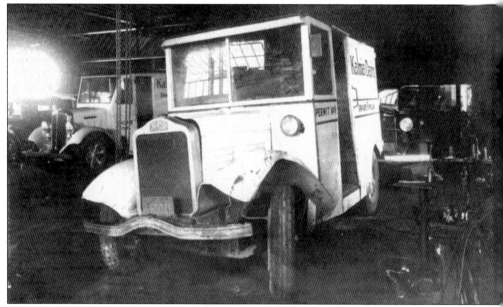

Kalmia Dairy began in 1922 when A. S. "Bert" Browning Jr. opened his dairy on Brevard Road where Hawthorne Hills is today. Around 1950, the dairy expanded into a plant on the Asheville Highway. The most memorable part of the dairy was the Kalmia Dairy Bar, where one could order food, especially desserts, with a scoop of heavenly fresh ice cream. (Photograph courtesy of Charlie King; Baker-Barber Collection, Community Foundation of Henderson County.)

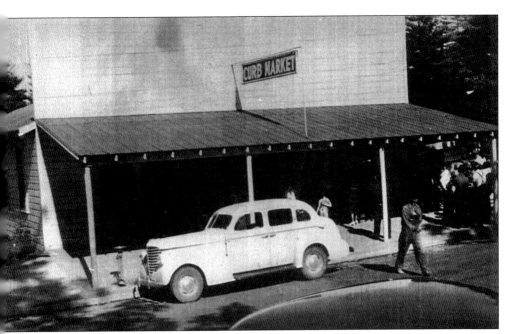

The Curb Market opened in an outdoor lot on Main Street c. 1924 and was incorporated in 1933 with each member owning a share of stock. In 1965, the present building on the corner of Church Street was erected. The Curb Market is a non-profit farmers' cooperative organization. Vendors, many of whom are third generation, must live in Henderson County, and only the goods from their farms may be sold. (Courtesy of Nancy Ball and the Curb Market.)

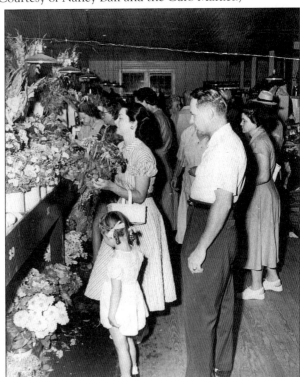

Pictured here is the inside of the Curb Market around 1950. The image shows the great variety of goods available. (Photograph courtesy of Hendersonville Chamber of Commerce; Baker-Barber Collection, Community Foundation of Henderson County.)

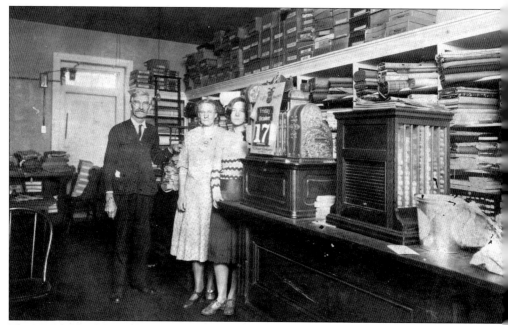

The M. M. Shepherd Store moved to 218 North Main Street in 1896. This interior photograph shows the shelves of dry goods that were part of their inventory. Appearing from left to right are an unidentified clerk, Susan Shepherd, and her daughter Ruth Shepherd. The Shepherd family recently restored the building, which remains in the family today. (Courtesy of Sue Shepherd Sneeringer.)

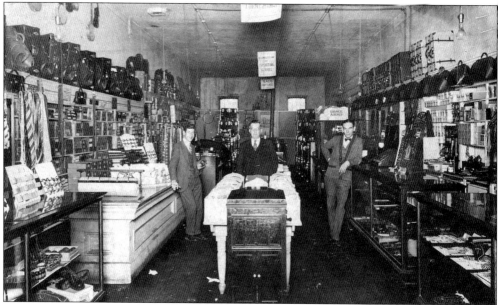

Shown here in this old photograph is the interior of Sherman's Sporting Goods Store. The store started in this building, where the seating area of Hannah Flanagan's restaurant is located today. It then moved to 340 Main Street before moving to its present location at 126 Main Street. From left to right are Louis Sherman, an unidentified clerk, and Anchell Gold. (Courtesy of Becky Sherman Banadyga.)

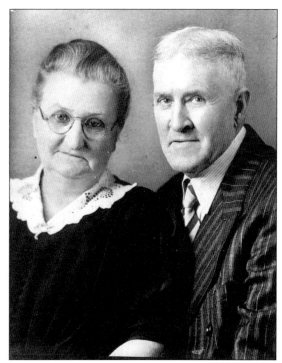

Pictured here are Glenn Xenophon Thompson and his wife, Leona Taylor Thompson, proprietors of Thompson's Produce on Seventh Avenue. Their homestead was on the corner of Duncan Hill Road and Seventh Avenue, now the location of Peggy's Ice Cream and Harry's Restaurant. The restaurant encompasses their original smokehouse. Both Piggy's and Harry's are run by fourth-generation Thompsons. (Courtesy of the Thompson family.)

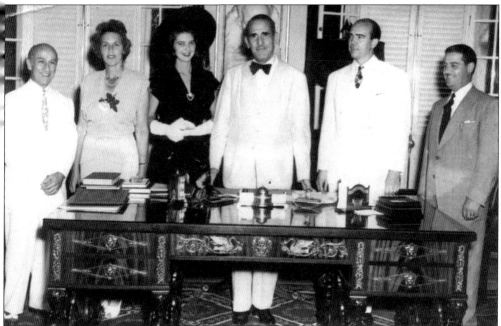

In this c. 1948 image, Joan Sample (third from left) is shown on a trip to Miami, which she won for being chosen queen of the Apple Harvest Festival. The tourism industry is important to Hendersonville's economy, and the Apple Harvest Festivals have always drawn visitors. The festival queen was chaperoned by Alice Andrews, seen in this photograph second from left, flanked by members of the Cuban Tourist Commission. (Courtesy of David W. Cooley and Hendersonville Chamber of Commerce.)

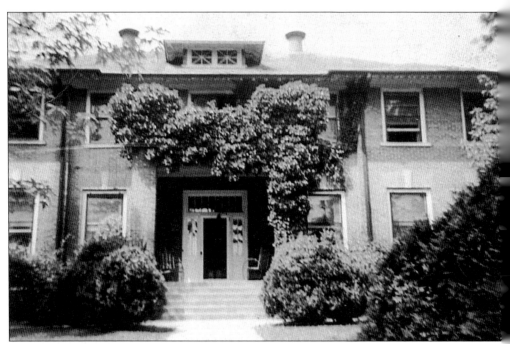

In 1912, Annie E. Patton donated land on Patton Avenue for a hospital. In 1925, the Trenholm Wing was added, and in 1938 the Nurses Home was completed. Patton Hospital is seen in this photograph, c. 1940. It had 4 wards and 12 private rooms. By 1917, the cost of a private room was $3.50 per day. (Courtesy of Patricia F. Sproles.)

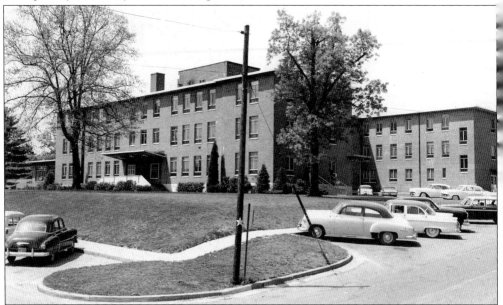

Seen here is the Margaret R. Pardee Hospital, dedicated in 1953. Ivor Pardee donated $100,000, and a bond issue of $250,000 was approved. With this seed money, financial assistance from the North Carolina Medical Care Commission, and assets from Patton Hospital, Pardee Hospital became a reality. It is named after an aunt of Ivor Pardee. This photograph was taken c. 1955. (Photograph by Ed Hunnicutt and courtesy of Hendersonville Chamber of Commerce.)

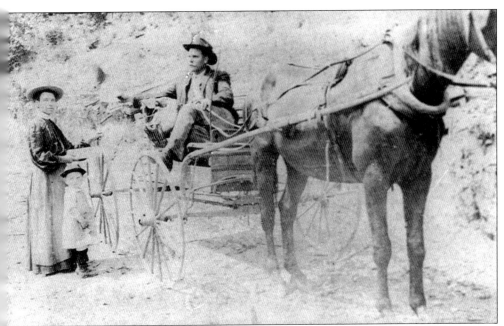

Pictured here in this extremely old and rare c. 1890 photograph is Robert Valentine Kuykendall, delivering mail to an unidentified woman and child. Kuykendall was an early postmaster with several routes both in Hendersonville and Flat Rock. Kuykendall was the great-great-great-grandson of pioneer and patriot Abraham Kuykendall who settled in this area in the late 18th century. (Courtesy of Charles Kuykendall.)

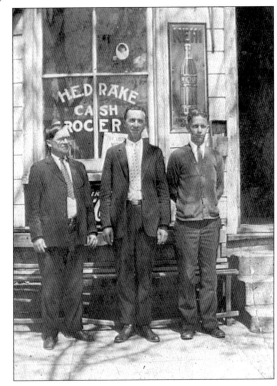

Shown here from left to right are Dick Sentelle, "Skin" Drake, and Preston Drake. They are in front of the H. E. Drake store on Main Street and First Avenue. (Courtesy of Jeff Miller.)

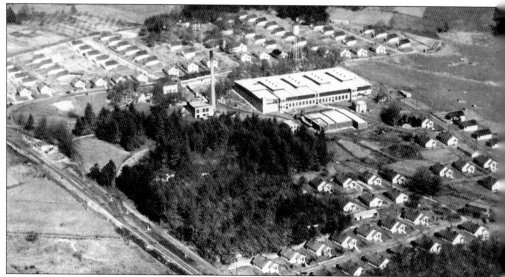

Capt. Ellison Adger Smyth founded Balfour Mills after retiring from a successful textile career. Bored with retirement, he established the mill two miles north of Hendersonville in about 1923. This photograph shows the mill and the mill village around it. Houses were owned by the mill and had either four or six rooms. Grace Gaillard remembers growing up there and catching the city bus to town. (Courtesy of Scottie M. Capell and Grace Gaillard.)

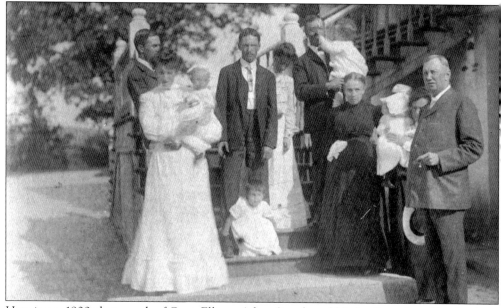

Here is a c. 1900 photograph of Capt. Ellison Adger Smyth and his family gathered by the front steps at Rock Hill. Shortly after purchasing the property, he changed the name to Connemara and painted the house green. Appearing from left to right are Lewis D. Blake, Annie Pierce Smyth Blake holding their unidentified child, James A. Smyth, with an unidentified child sitting on a step, Mary Smyth McKay, A. F. McKissick, holding an unidentified child, Julie Gambrill Smyth, Jane Adger Smyth (partially hidden) holding her unidentified child, and Capt. Ellison Adger Smyth. (Photograph courtesy of Carl Sandburg Home, National Historic Site, National Park Service; Julianne Heggoy Collection.)

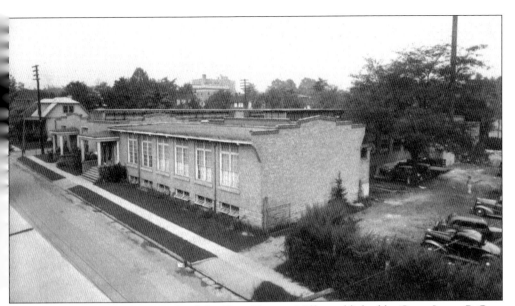

Seen here is a c. 1940 photograph of the Grey Hosiery Mill, established by Capt. James P. Grey in 1915. In 1965, the mill was sold to Holt Hosiery Mills Corp., and closed in 1967. The Mill Company purchased the building in 1977 with the intention of making it into a market for arts and crafts. Today an organization is working to establish a fine-arts center in the old mill. (Courtesy of Charlie King.)

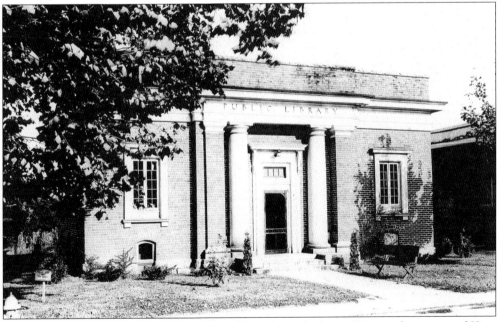

Pictured here is the first Hendersonville Public Library built in 1914 on the corner of King Street East and Fourth Avenue. Land for the building was donated by Capt. Marion Toms, and funds for the library building were personally donated by Andrew Carnegie. The library was then called the Andrew Carnegie Library. On opening day, everyone was asked to bring a book to donate, which resulted in a collection of 514 books. This building is now the Greater Hendersonville Chamber of Commerce. (Courtesy of Charlie King.)

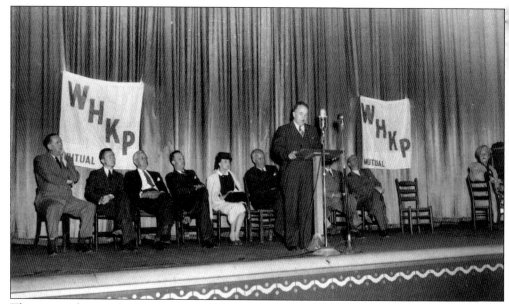

This image depicts the October 24, 1946, inaugural broadcast of radio station WHKP on the stage of the Carolina Theater. Pictured from left to right are Mayor Al Edwards, A. D. Cornea, G. C. Richardson Sr., M. M. Redden Sr., Mrs. John Forrest, William Egerton, Ralph Martin, Rev. Dr. Ted Heyman, Clarence Morgan (mayor of Asheville), and Kate Dotson. (Photograph courtesy of WHKP; Baker-Barber Collection, Community Foundation of Henderson County.)

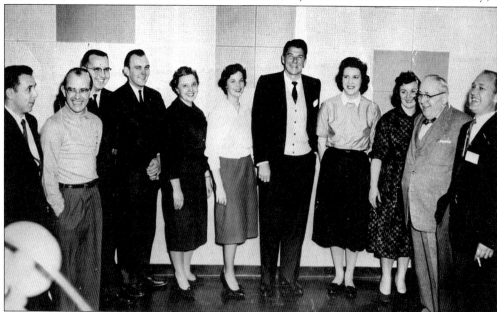

On February 24, 1960, Ronald Reagan paid a visit to Hendersonville and to WHKP. Reagan was employed by the General Electric Company at the time and was visiting plants as part of his public relations duties. He participated in a forum program. Appearing from left to right are Jim Northington, Charlie Renfrow, Bill Edmundson, Art Cooley, Jo Kuykendall, Henrietta Hensley, Ronald Reagan, Betty Lee, Mary Ashe, Don Gilmore, and Kermit Edney. (Courtesy of WHKP.)

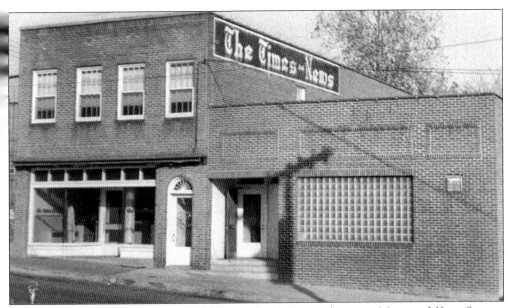

Pictured here is the *Times-News* building on Sixth Avenue between Main and King Streets. After the newspaper moved to their present home on Four Seasons Boulevard, this building was used as the Hendersonville Police Department. It has recently been demolished. (Courtesy of David W. Cooley.)

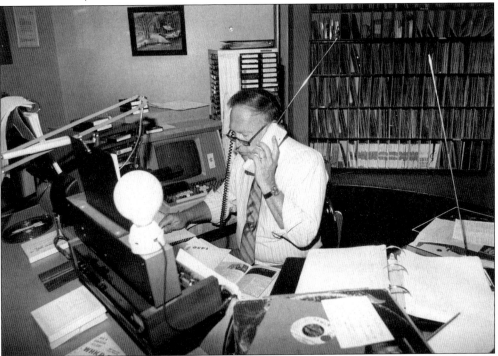

This is a photograph of Kermit Edney at work in the WHKP studios. He was a favorite on-air personality, and generations grew up listening to him on the radio. One of his pet projects was the Community Foundation of Henderson County, which he helped to found. Kermit Edney also was an author.

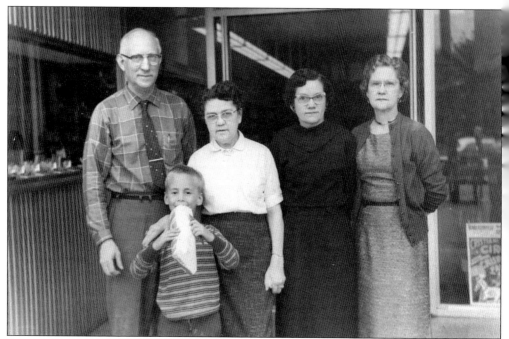

French's Jewelers on Main Street served downtown Hendersonville for many years. It opened in the 1940s and finally closed in the 1980s. Appearing in this 1956 photograph are from left to right Charlie French Sr., Marjie French, Drucilla Baltisberger, May Ledbetter, and French Trembly (in the front). Mr. French often serviced the clock on the First Citizens Bank building. (Courtesy of Annie Sue French Foster.)

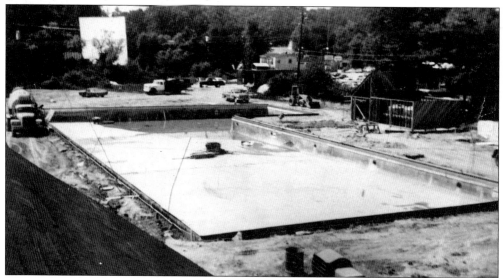

This photograph shows construction of the city's Patton Pool in about 1977. In the distance, the screen at the Hendersonville Drive-In is visible. This theater, along with the Joy Drive-In on Spartanburg Highway, entertained dating couples and families for years. According to former projectionist John Rheinhart, when he worked at the Hendersonville Drive-In, double features would start at dusk, after which cars wanting to leave could depart prior to the adult movie showing later. (Courtesy of the City of Hendersonville.)

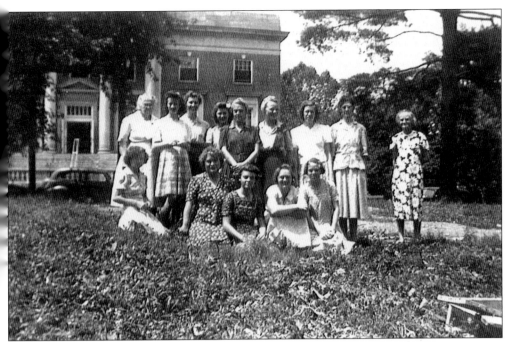

Shown here is the staff of Millers Cleaning c. 1930 when the company moved to its present site. Norman W. Miller started the business in 1915 when he purchased a "pressing club" from H. Patterson. It remains in the family today. In the background, city hall is visible. (Courtesy of Jeff Miller.)

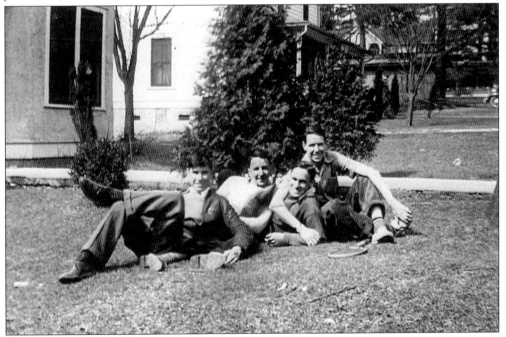

This picture shows four local boys hanging out on King Street, c. 1939. Shown in this picture are from left to right Louie Hesterly, Aiken Pace, Tom Allison, and Bert Miller of Millers Cleaning. In the background are houses lining King Street. (Courtesy of Jeff Miller.)

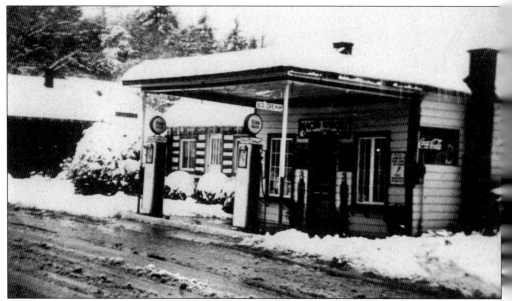

Seen in this c. 1930 photograph is the old Mace General Store. The older part of the store and the adjoining home were made of logs. It stood at Busy Bend on Kanuga Road. The store, owned by the Mace family, sold everything a person could need from ice cream to gasoline. (Courtesy of Phillip Mace.)

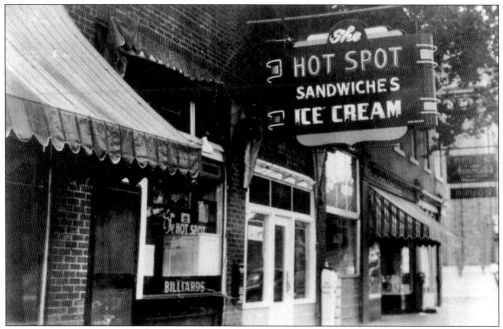

This is the Hot Spot at 337 Main Street. Frank Edney bought the restaurant in 1946 and ran it for nearly 30 years. The Hot Spot catered to men and served beer, while the Blue Bird next door shared the same kitchen, catered to ladies, and served ice cream. The Hot Spot opened at 5 a.m. and was a gathering place for farmers, deliverymen, and businessmen, including Kermit Edney and the Breakfast Bunch, who stopped by before they opened the radio station, WHKP. (Courtesy of Jimmy Edney.)

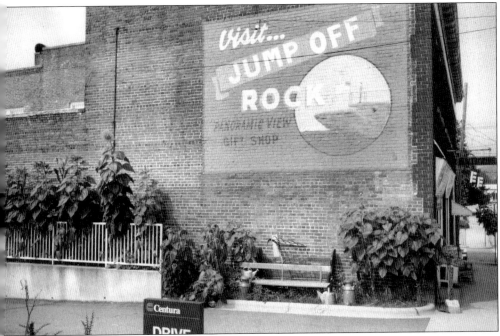

Shown here on Third Avenue is the Brooks Building built around 1920 with the classic "Jump Off Rock" mural. For many years, the building housed Clifton's Restaurant and the Smoke Shop, which were businesses owned by the Shipman Brothers. It remains in the family today. (Courtesy of Eddie Shipman.)

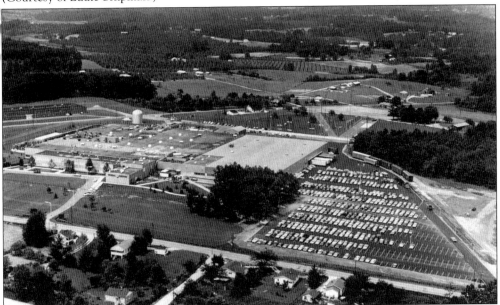

Rumors abounded in 1954 that a major new company was about to come to town. The announcement was made in the Skyland Hotel that General Electric outdoor lighting and traffic control departments would relocate here from Massachusetts. The plant was a boon to the Hendersonville economy. For every person who moved here, nine local workers were hired. The plant is located in East Flat Rock and has proven to be a wonderful neighbor.

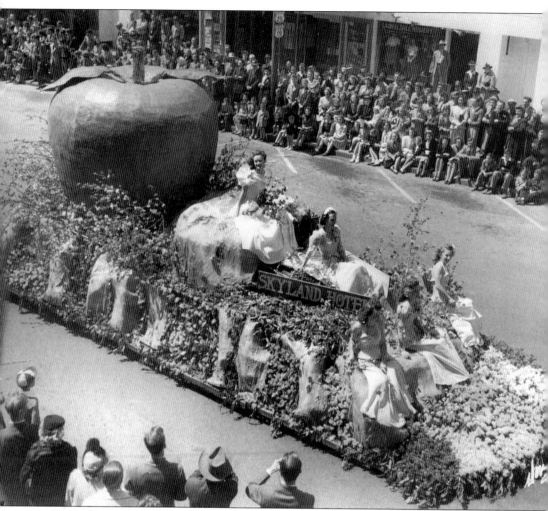

Pictured here is the Skyland Hotel float in the Apple Parade of 1950. The apple industry began with William Mills, thought to be the first white settler in the county. He found the mountain valleys receptive to growing all types of fruit trees, especially apples. It was a hard business when hauling had to be done by wagon. Gerber Products came to Skyland in 1959 and helped revolutionize the business. Henderson County is one of the biggest producers of apples in the country. (Courtesy Hendersonville Chamber of Commerce.)

Six

FESTIVALS AND THE ARTS

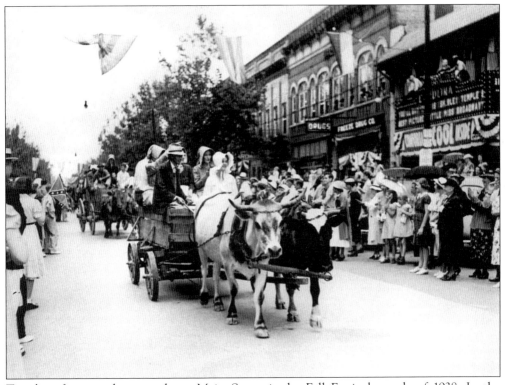

Traveling from south to north on Main Street is the Fall Festival parade of 1938. In the background is the Carolina Theater, which at the time, was showing the best picture of the year, *Little Miss Broadway*, starring Shirley Temple. Hendersonville has always loved a parade. Even before apple festivals, there were parades on Main Street for almost any reason. (Photograph courtesy of Hendersonville Chamber of Commerce; Baker-Barber Collection, Community Foundation of Henderson County.)

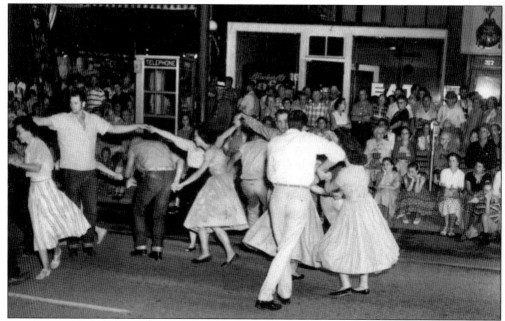

Hendersonville Chamber of Commerce started street dances at the end of World War I. During the 1940s, photographer Jody Barber was a caller. The venue for street dancing was Main Street, but for a time, they were held on the tennis courts in Boyd Park. Another form of dancing, clogging, was also very popular. Hendersonville's Echo Mountain Cloggers were world champions. (Photograph by Bill Gulley and courtesy of Hendersonville Chamber of Commerce.)

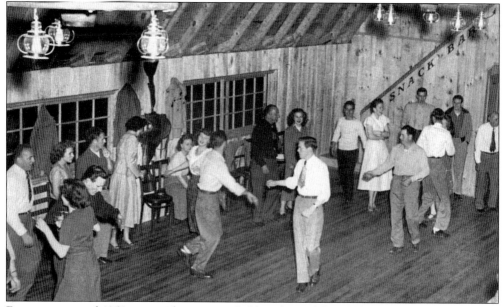

For a time around 1950, square dances were held in the Saddle Club barn that now is home to Hendersonville Little Theater. Appearing in this photograph are Pat Reese (in the forefront, right of center) and David W. Cooley (second from left in a dark shirt) with unidentified dancers in the square dance club. (Courtesy of Hendersonville Chamber of Commerce.)

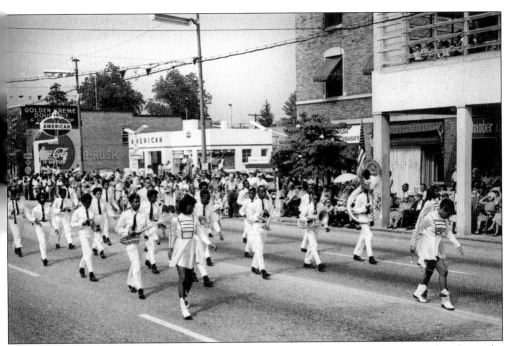

Shown here c. 1962 is the Ninth Avenue School's "Tiger Band" marching in a local parade. (Courtesy of Hendersonville High School Alumni Association.)

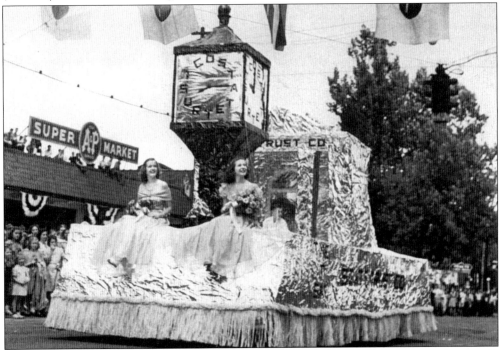

Everyone loves a parade! This is a 1949 photograph of the King Apple Parade traveling north on Main Street as they pass the A and P. The First State Bank and Trust was the principle bank in town at the time and their float carries a replica of the clock that adorns their building. (Photograph by Richard Wooten and courtesy of David W. Cooley.)

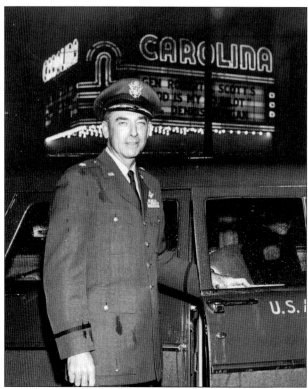

Pictured here in 1945 is Gen. Robert Scott, author of *God is my Co-Pilot*. He is standing in front of the Carolina Theater where the movie version of his book was showing. General Scott was there by way of the Chamber of Commerce's invitation to entertain at their annual meeting held at Hendersonville High School. He brought with him the "Singing Sergeants" and the "Strolling Strings." (Courtesy of Hendersonville Chamber of Commerce.)

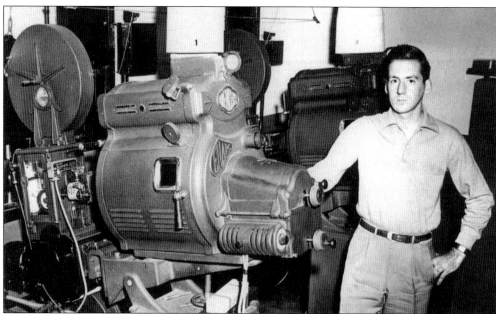

Shown here in 1955 is Arthur M. Huggins, chief projectionist at the Fox Theater. Built as the Queen Theater and later named the Fox, it was designed by Erle Stilwell and built in 1915 at 434 North Main Street. The building now houses Goldsmith Jewelers. Other theaters were the Rialto on Main and Third Streets and the Palace on Main Street and Fifth Avenue. The Palace is thought to be Hendersonville's first movie theater. (Courtesy of Arthur M. Huggins.)

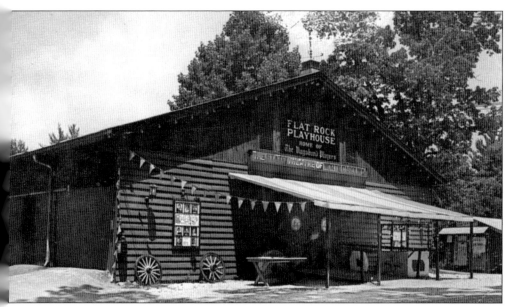

Mention the theater, and Flat Rock Playhouse comes to mind. It is the State Theater of North Carolina and was the first summer stock theater in the state when it opened in Rhett's Mill in 1940. In 1952, after a successful building drive, a permanent theater building was erected on the present site of the playhouse, shown here in this 1961 postcard. It is one of the best summer stock theaters in the country. (Courtesy of Eddie Shipman.)

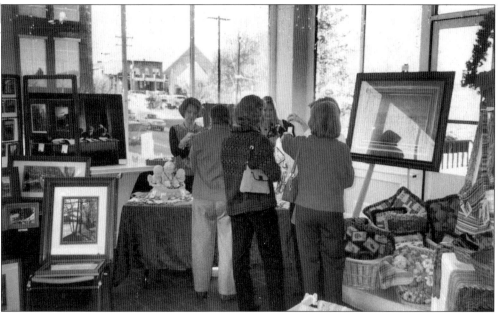

This is a recent photograph of the Arts Center. Located on the second floor of the Skyland Hotel on Main Street, the Arts Center opened under the auspices of Four Seasons Arts Council in 1991 and has enjoyed continued success since then. The gallery is on the second floor and balcony of the Skyland Hotel. This photograph shows the Art Market, now a yearly event for holiday shopping. (Courtesy of Sherry Preisler and the Arts Center.)

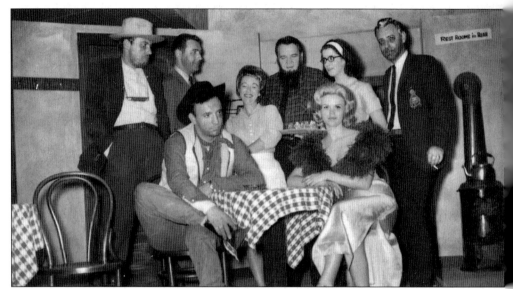

Established c. 1966 by a small group of theater lovers, Hendersonville Little Theater is the oldest community theater in the city. The theater's first production *Bus Stop*, staged in a rented warehouse using a set designed by Jan Clausing (a retired art director from Radio City Music Hall in New York), is depicted here. The cast included Diane and Doug Brooks, Patty Johnson, Jennette Story, Bob Ford, Don Dixon, and Philip and Frank Elliott. (Courtesy of Hendersonville Little Theater.)

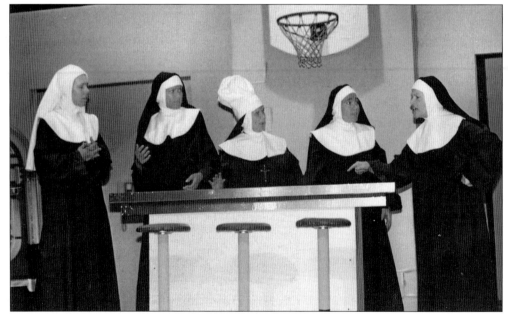

In 1969, Hendersonville Little Theater moved to the old Hendersonville Saddle Club on State Street and transformed the building into a theater seating 121. The first play in the "Barn" was *Picnic*. Appearing here onstage in *Nunsense* are from left to right Chrissy Eide, Carol Duermit, Rosie O'Brien, Lisa Abeling, and Nancy Colangione. This community theater is an all-volunteer organization and stages four to six productions a year. (Courtesy of Hendersonville Little Theater.)

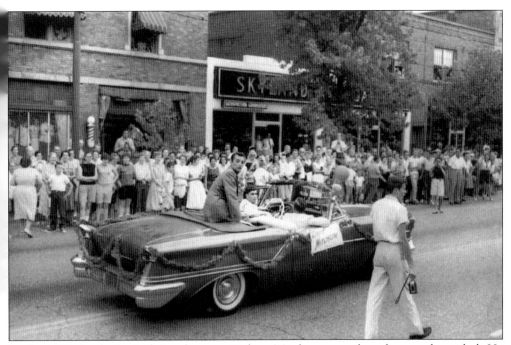

In the 1953 Apple Festival Parade, actor Robert Mitchum served as the grand marshal. He was in the area filming *Thunder Road*. The movie was filmed along the French Broad River on Route 191. He stayed at the Grove Park Inn but frequently came to Hendersonville. (Courtesy of David W. Cooley and the Hendersonville Chamber of Commerce.)

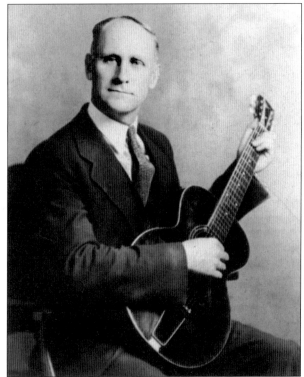

Appearing in this portrait is Otis Kuykendall who gave Jimmie Rogers (the father of country music) his first real "gig" in Hendersonville in the 1920s. Kuykendall and Rogers were the first act to play on the newly formed WWNC radio out of Asheville. Hendersonville was a mecca for music of all genres for many years, including big bands and country music. (Courtesy of Charles Kuykendall.)

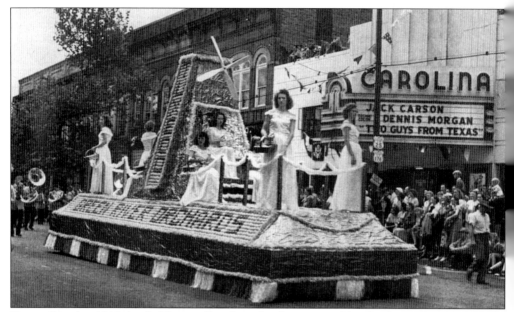

Pictured in this 1948 Apple Harvest Parade is the float entered by the Green River Orchards. This photograph was taken on Labor Day as the parade passed Carolina Theater. Showing at the theater was *Two Guys From Texas* in "Techno Color." To the left of the theater is where the Mast General Store is located today. At one time, Mast General Store was a hardware store on the lower level with a funeral parlor upstairs. (Photograph by Richard Wooten and courtesy of Lynn Martin.)

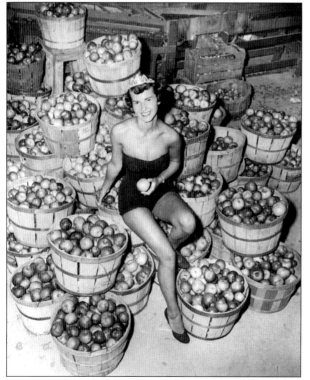

Shown in this 1955 photograph is the queen of the Apple Blossom Festival, Joan Sample. The first festival was held in 1947 in the springtime. The next year, the festival was moved to the fall and was called the Apple Harvest Festival, and the year after that, it became the North Carolina Apple Festival. (Photograph courtesy of Hendersonville Chamber of Commerce; Baker-Barber Collection, Community Foundation of Henderson County.)

Shown in this c. 1960 picture is Bob Keechan, known as "Captain Kangaroo," with David Cooley (left) and Ann Cooley Farrell (right) on his lap. Keechan was the spokesman for Gerber Baby Food and participated in the Apple Festival. Playing Captain Kangaroo, Keechan went to the children's home that night and tucked them into bed . . . Christmas in September! (Courtesy: David W. Cooley.)

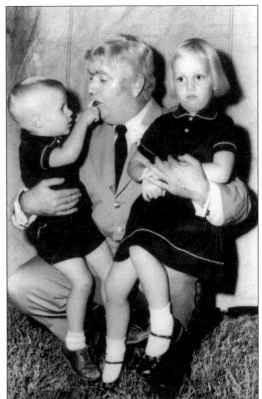

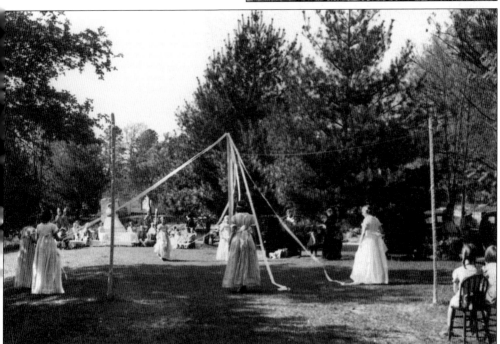

This photograph shows a Maypole celebration from 1939 at Immaculata School at 1133 Oakland Street. (Courtesy of Immaculata Catholic School.)

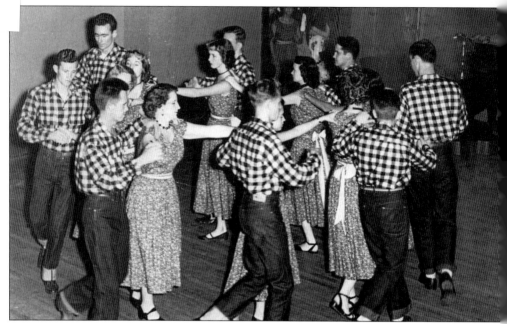

Square dancing has been one of the most popular pastimes in Hendersonville for many years. Seen here is a 1953 photograph of unidentified dancers enjoying themselves at one of their functions. Hendersonville gained national attention as the "Dancingest Town in America." (Courtesy of Hendersonville Chamber of Commerce.)

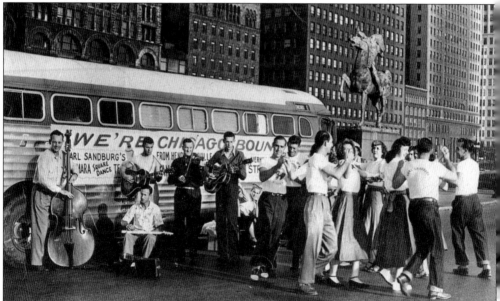

Shown here is the Connemara Dance Team in a 1948 photograph. They were on a trip to Chicago to compete in the Chicago Railroad Fair. The team won the honor to compete by coming in first in the square-dance competition at the Apple Harvest Festival. "Apple Queen" Juanita Thompson accompanied the team. Also with them was the Vernon Rogers Blue Sky Rangers Band. Traffic in the Chicago Loop stopped to listen to their music. On the bus is their banner, "We're Chicago Bound." (Courtesy of Geraldine Collis.)

Seven
Sports and Recreation

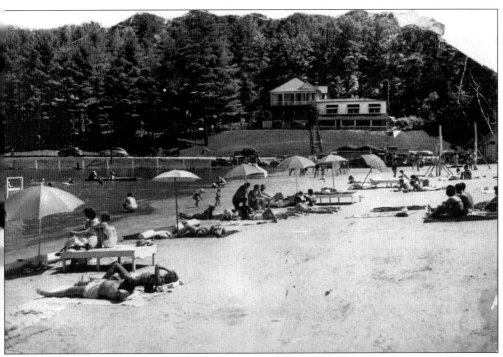

Pictured here is the Laurel Park Inn and Cottages. There were two lakes, the Laurel and the Rhododendron, connected by a canal. These were popular places to swim and socialize. In the evening, there was dancing to big-band music at the pavilion. A rail line, called the "dummy line," ran between Main Street and the lakes. It was called that name because it could not turn around. (Courtesy of Lynn Blackwell.)

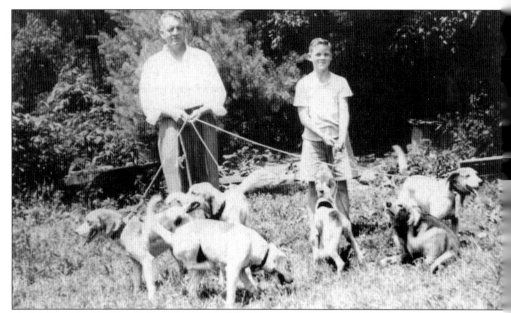

In this 1944 image are Ulysses Mace and his son, Philip, with their Walker fox hounds. The family owned a store on Kanuga Road at "busy bend." Three of the dogs were Ranger, Bob, and Bell. The dog on the far right was a "treeing dog" named Danger. Mr. Mace bought and sold most things including, as the story goes, Danger. The dog was sent to South Carolina, and a month later, Danger found his way home to Hendersonville. He lived with his family until the age of 18. (Courtesy of Phillip Mace.)

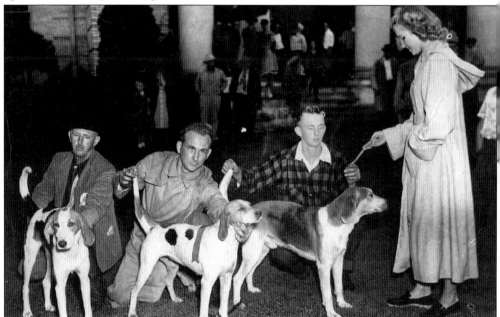

This is a charming photograph of competition winners at the 1949 Apple Festival. The Blue Ridge Hounds are the winners of the ribbons, which are shown presented on the historic Henderson County Courthouse lawn by Apple Festival queen Juanita Thompson. (Photograph by Horace Mann and courtesy of Hendersonville Chamber of Commerce.)

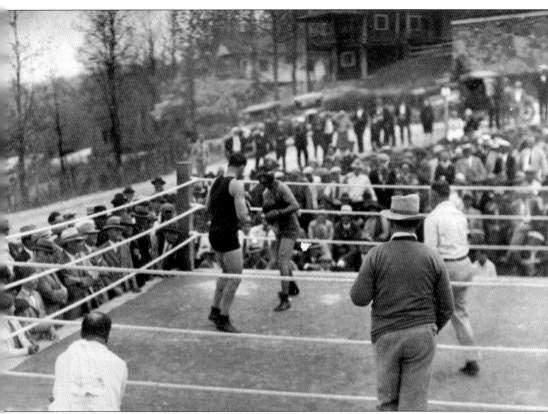

Pictured here is boxer Jack Dempsey in the sparring ring at Indian Cave Lodge. Dempsey and his wife, actress Estelle Taylor, were invited to Hendersonville as a promotion for Laurel Park, which was being developed as an exclusive resort. They stayed at the Kentucky Home on Fourth Avenue West and Washington Street. They often walked through town and chatted with residents. Dempsey ruled the boxing ring between 1919 and 1926 and was a major contributor to the Golden Age of Sports. His contemporaries were Babe Ruth and Lou Gehrig (baseball), Bobby Jones and Walter Hagen (golf), Bill Tilden and Suzanne Lenglen (tennis), Red Grange and The Four Horsemen (football), Johny Weissmuller (swimming), and Man O'War (horse racing) to name a few. He lost his title in 1926 to Gene Tunny in front of more than 100,000 fans. Returning to his hotel room, bloody and beaten, he said to his wife, "Honey, I forgot to duck." He died at 87 in 1983. A full-page obituary was published in the *New York Times*, written by noted sports writer Red Smith. When Dempsey left Hendersonville, "Young" Stribling was waiting to take his place. Called the "Georgia Boy Wonder," he loved this area. (Photograph courtesy of Charlie King; Baker Barber Collection Community Foundation of Henderson County.)

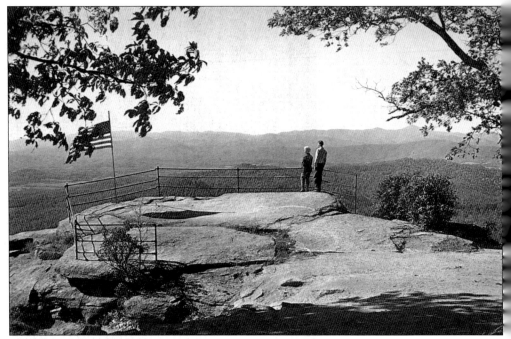

Pictured on this post card is Jump Off Rock. Legend has it a young Indian chief fell in love with an Indian maiden. Jump Off Rock was their meeting place. When the warrior went on the war path, his young love went to the rock every day to watch for his return. He never returned. Heartbroken, she plunged to her death below. Native Americans believed that when the moon was full, the maiden could still be heard calling her beloved.

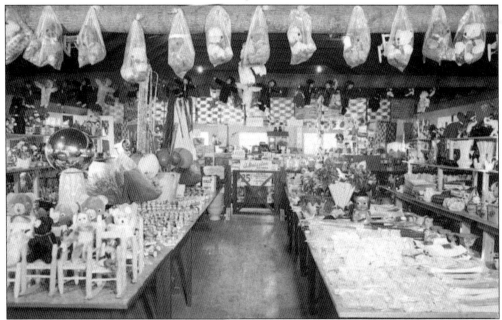

Here a postcard shows the interior of the old gift shop at the entrance to Jump Off Rock, which is located on Jump Off Mountain, just west of Hendersonville in Laurel Park. The postcard advertises novelties and souvenirs. (Courtesy of Eddie Shipman.)

Pictured here is Mary Helen Boyd Zimmerman in 1956. She is shown about to present the winning rider with a blue ribbon. The first horse show was held on Hendersonville High School's football field in the 1930s. It then moved to the Western North Carolina Fairgrounds where East Henderson High School now stands. The horse show was a big event and greatly anticipated each year. (Photograph by Harris and courtesy of Hendersonville Chamber of Commerce.)

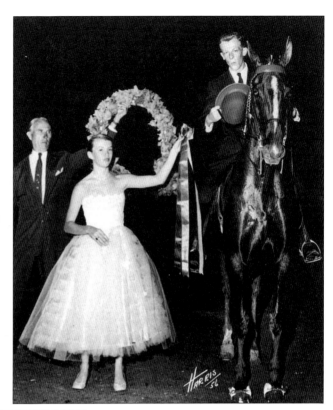

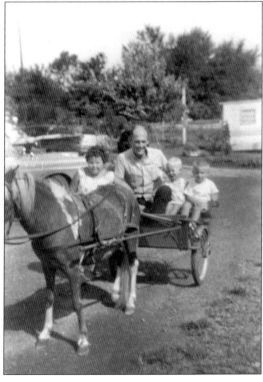

Taking a ride in a cart pulled by Penny the pony are from left to right Cathy Ellington, Calvin Ellington, Debbie Creasman, and Mike Williams. This picture was taken at the Garren Recreation Area on Kanuga Road. (Courtesy of Cathy Garren Ellington.)

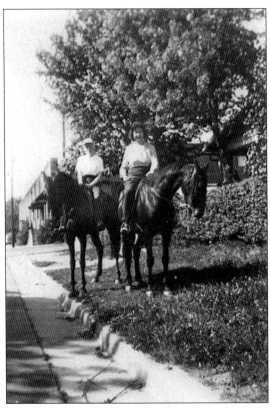

Sue Brookshire (left) and Orlette Drake, daughter of H. E. Drake, enjoy a ride around town c. 1939. They are posing in front of the Drake home on Church Street. Becker's Bakery, now the Samovar Café, is visible in the background. The bakery started on Seventh Avenue and later moved to the corner of Church and Barnwell Streets. They offered home delivery and advertised their signature "butternut bread" on the side panels of their trucks. (Courtesy of Jeff Miller.)

The top of Pinnacle Mountain was a popular place for hiking and picnicking. In a c. 1904 photograph, M. M. Shepherd is shown on the left with his brother Tom. (Courtesy of Sue Shepherd Sneeringer.)

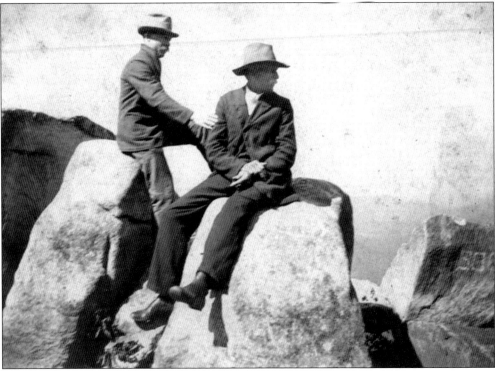

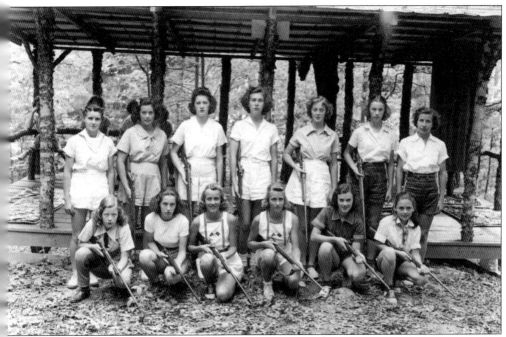

This is a photograph of unidentified young ladies at Camp Greystone during firearms training. The young lady standing on the far left must have plans for the evening—note the hair curlers. The Hendersonville area has been known for its summer camps for many years. The pleasant climate, clear lakes, and healthy outdoor activities are a draw for young people from all over the country.

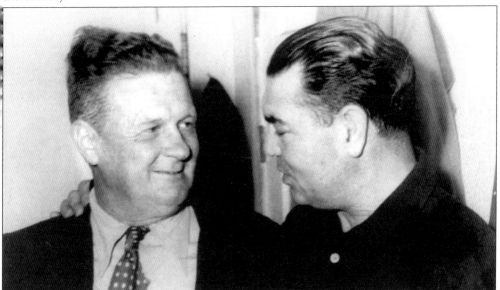

Taken c. 1950, this photograph shows professional boxer, the affable Jack Dempsey (right), with Walter B. Smith. Dempsey was back in Hendersonville for a visit after spending time here in the mid-1920s. Walter B. Smith was the son of Laurel Park developer W. A. Smith. Walt was considered quite a town character, sometimes calling the president of the United States from the Hot Spot on Main Street. (Courtesy of Jimmy Edney.)

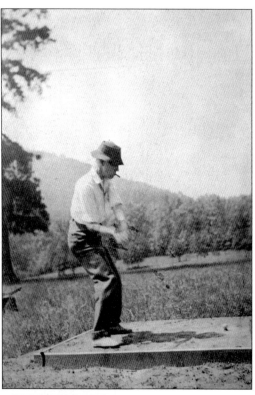

Pictured on a tee box of the area's first golf course on record is Lewis D. Blake, husband of Captain Smyth's daughter, Annie. The golf course was built by Capt. Ellison Adger Smyth on his farm, Connemara. This was a nine-hole course with gravel tee boxes. To make it the correct length, some holes had to be played twice from different teeing areas. (Courtesy of Carl Sandburg Home, National Historic Society, National Parks Service.)

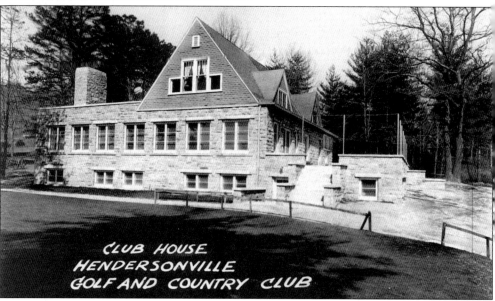

This is the old clubhouse of what was then called the Hendersonville Golf and Country Club, now the Hendersonville Country Club. A residence on the Ransier pony farm was used as the first clubhouse. It underwent several expansions throughout the years. During construction in 1987, a devastating fire destroyed the building shown here. A new clubhouse was constructed and opened nine months later. (Photograph courtesy of Hendersonville Chamber of Commerce; Baker-Barber Collection, Community Foundation of Henderson County.)

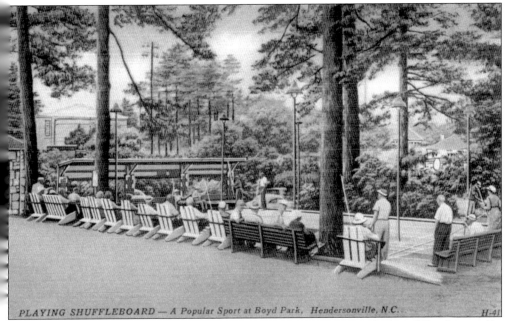

PLAYING SHUFFLEBOARD — A Popular Sport at Boyd Park, Hendersonville, N.C.   H-41

From the time Floridians discovered the cool air and pleasant summer climate of Hendersonville, shuffleboard has been a popular pastime. This is a postcard showing the shuffleboard courts at Boyd Park. The park was named after Bert Boyd.

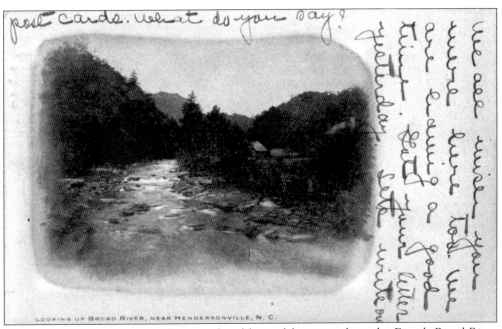

A postcard dated 1906 shows the rugged and beautiful terrain along the French Broad River near Hendersonville. The French Broad River is the third-oldest river in the world behind the Nile and the New, all of which flow north. Both the French Broad and the New flow through North Carolina. This postcard, with a one-cent stamp attached, was sent home from a happy tourist to a friend in Jersey City, New Jersey.

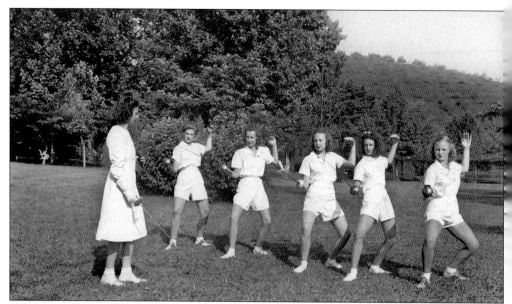

This is an unidentified group of young lady campers at Camp Greystone. In addition to the art of fencing, campers learned archery, firearms, swimming, boating, and horsemanship. This photograph was taken c. 1950. (Courtesy of Hendersonville Chamber of Commerce.)

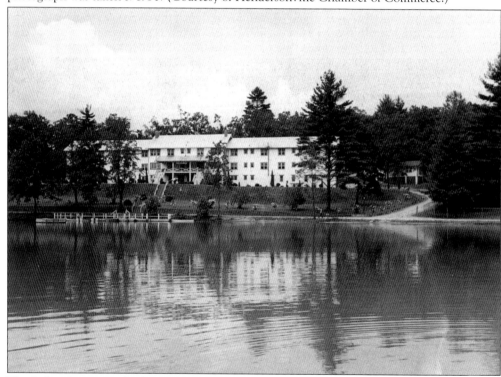

The Lakeside Inn was built c. 1945 overlooking Lake Osceola. It then became Camp Lakeside, a camp predominantly for Jewish American children from Florida. It was then renamed Camp Mountain Lake. The building is now gone, but the property is owned by a former camper who plans to build on the site overlooking the lake. (Courtesy of Todd Leoni.)

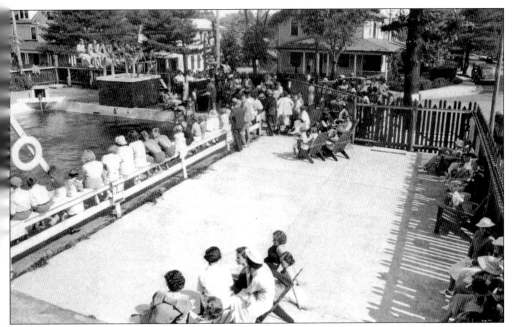

Pictured here is the Weeping Willow Pool, built by J. K. Livingston. Located on the corner of Third Avenue and Washington Street, it was a popular place in the summer months. J. K. Livingston also promoted bands and dances. He ran Tracy's and the Greyhound Bus Station. His son, "Buster," had his own successful band. (Photograph courtesy of Hendersonville Chamber of Commerce; Baker-Barber Collection, Community Foundation of Henderson County.)

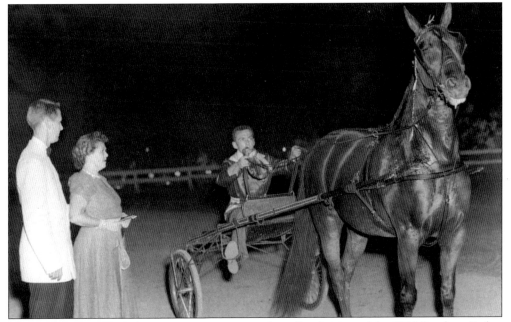

This is a picture of Jack Atwater participating in the sulky division of the 1954 Roadster Stakes held at the Hendersonville Horse Show. The show was a very popular event, and contestants trained and worked all year for it. (Photograph by Harris and courtesy of Hendersonville Chamber of Commerce.)

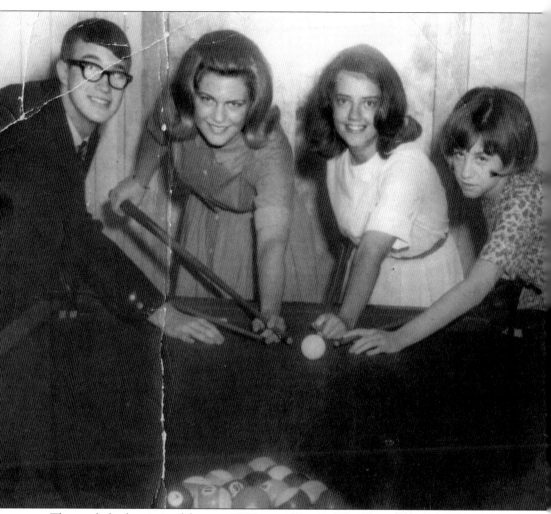

The pool sharks pictured here c. 1965 are officers of the Teen Canteen. This canteen was operated as a joint venture between the city and the community as a place for teens to go. Located in Boyd Park where the firehouse is today, the Canteen had a dance area, pool tables, booths, and a jukebox. Local combos played at the dances, and teens were required to clock in and out so parents could keep track of their children. For some years prior to this, there was a Teen Canteen in the area below the sidewalk known as "The Underground" on the corner of Fourth Avenue West and Main Street. From left to right are Mac Bennett, Linda Higdon, Diane Carpenter, and Carolyn Johnson. (Courtesy of Charlie King.)

Eight
PEOPLE

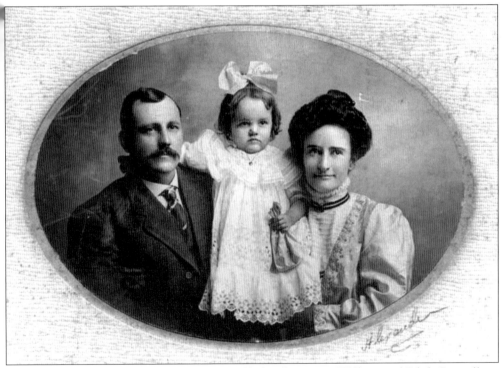

Here is a lovely portrait of an old Hendersonville family. George William and Edith Connell are pictured with their daughter, Reina, c. 1908. (Courtesy of David W. Cooley.)

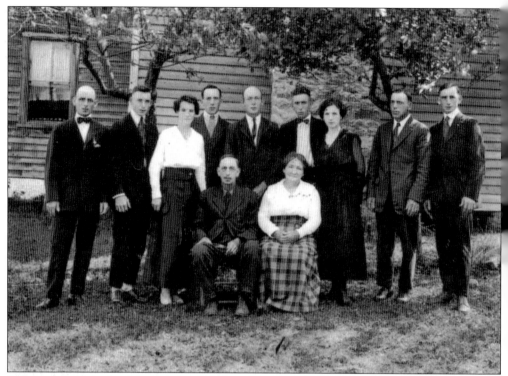

This is a photograph of the family of Nathan "Tete" Drake and Emma Anders Drake (seated). Sons in the photograph are from left to right J. Fanning Drake, Clayton Drake, Ned Drake, J. Mitchell Drake, Flave Drake, Russell Drake, and one unidentified gentleman. The daughters, from left to right, are Nannie Drake Brock and Jesse Drake Pressley. (Courtesy of Ellen H. Drake.)

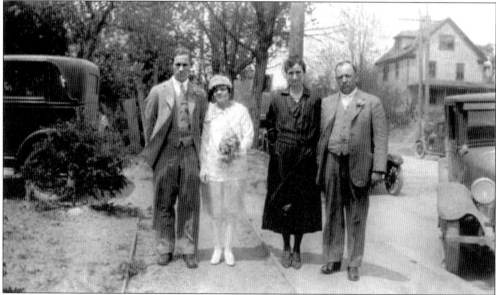

Pictured on their wedding day are Arthur Cooley and his bride Reina Connell with her mother Edith and father George W. Connell. The photograph was taken c. 1930 on Church Street near Shepherd's Funeral Home. (Courtesy of Dave and Art Cooley.)

Shown here c. 1905 are the daughters of Frank and Ella Stepp; Emma is on the left, and Flossie is on the right. Emma was a seamstress at several stores in Hendersonville, including Ruth Originals. Ruth Originals, located on Main Street, was started by Ruth Combs c. 1949. Patterns were cut, and housewives would pick up disassembled pieces, sew them together at home, and return the completed clothing to the shop for payment. (Courtesy of Jo Ann Stepp Fain.)

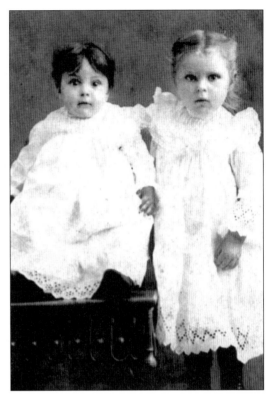

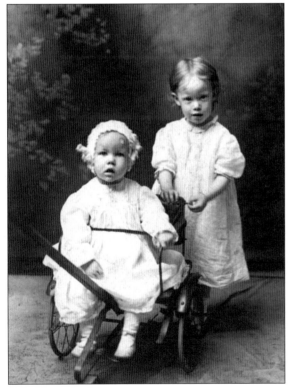

Looking quite the little angels around 1915 are Ruth (standing) and Katherine Shepherd, the daughters of M. M. and Susan Shepherd. (Courtesy of Sue Shepherd Sneeringer.)

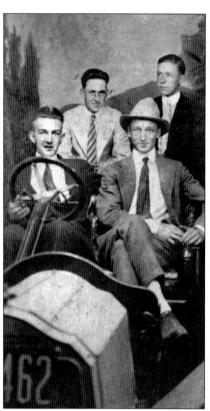

Men about town pose for a picture. In the first row, from left to right are Ben Williams and Obbie Smith. In the back row, from left to right are Harry Williams and Lee Whitmire. (Courtesy of Sue Shepherd Sneeringer.)

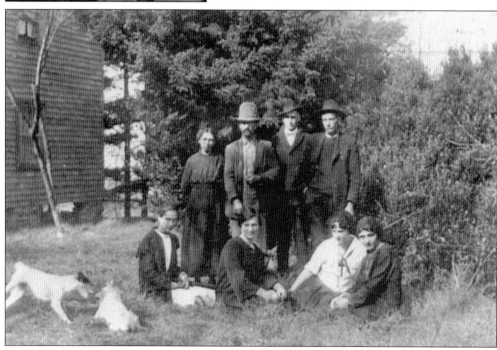

Pictured around 1936 is the Drake family at their home place on Willow Mountain. Standing at the far left is Viola Drake with unidentified family members. (Courtesy of Deborah Summey.)

Pictured at a family gathering from left to right are the following: (first row) Tunie Garren, Solomon Briggman (Brigg) Drake Jr., Kathleen Drake, and Lucy Drake; (second row) Charlie Garren (holding the dog, Patty), and Solomon Drake. (Courtesy of Barbara Peace Lohman.)

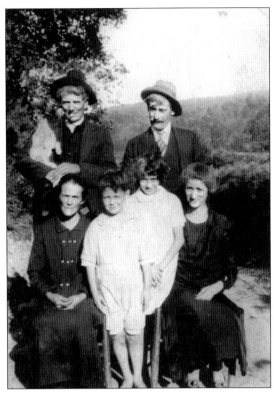

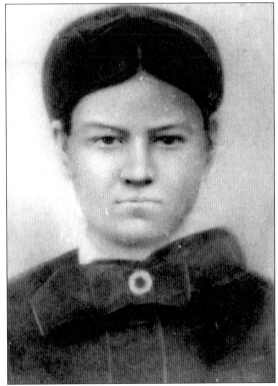

When the Drake and Garren's children were young, they heard more than once about an Indian chief in the family. This is a photograph of Rachael Betsy Sentelle, thought to be the daughter of that chief. She was the grandmother of Barbara Peace Lohman and Geraldine Collis. Born in Transylvania County c. 1857, she married William Brown of Madison County and they moved to Valley Hill. (Courtesy of Barbara Peace Lohman and Geraldine Collis.)

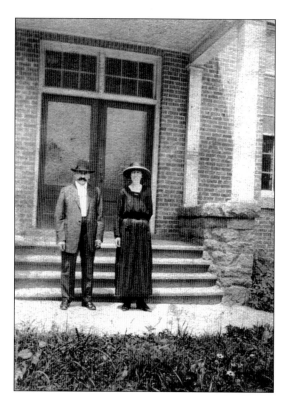

Standing in front of Grey Hosiery Mill c. 1918 are Frank O. Stepp and his wife, Ella Cagle Stepp. The Stepps lived across the street on the corner of Grove Street and Fourth Avenue. They owned the City Market butcher shop at 510 Seventh Avenue East from 1921 to 1926. (Courtesy of Jo Ann Stepp Fain.)

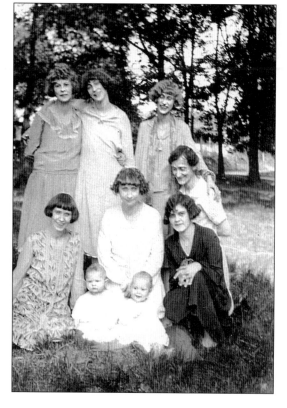

Pictured here is the French family on an outing. At the top, from left to right are unknown, Lennis French Bell, Nell French Parsons; (middle) Lennis Bolton French; (bottom) Pauline French Meak, Mattie Sue French, and Marjie Stowers French. The babies are C. B. French and Robert Meak. (Courtesy of Annie Sue Foster.)

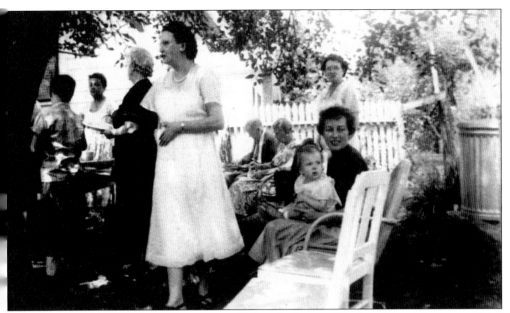

This picture shows a summer garden party c. 1955 at the home of Paul and Vernia Justus on Third Avenue East where the north entrance to Henderson County Courthouse is today. Standing from left to right are unidentified, Dahlia Clouse, Vera Justus, Gussie Justus Honeycutt, and unidentified. Seated from left to right are an unidentified man and woman, Sarah Heatherly Clouse, and infant Sarita Clouse. (Courtesy of Judy Clouse Loveland.)

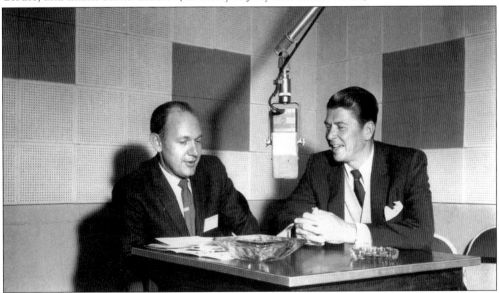

Photographed here in 1960 is Ronald Reagan, then president of the Screen Actors Guild. He was in Hendersonville to promote General Electric. Reagan is being interviewed by Kermit Edney on WHKP, where Reagan answered questions totally impromptu that were called in by listeners. Edney said later this was one of the easiest interviews he ever conducted. Kermit Edney was born in Hendersonville and attended Rosa Edwards School. Later he became an admired and loved broadcaster whose *Good Morning Man* theme song on WHKP was "On the Sunny Side of the Street." (Courtesy of WHKP.)

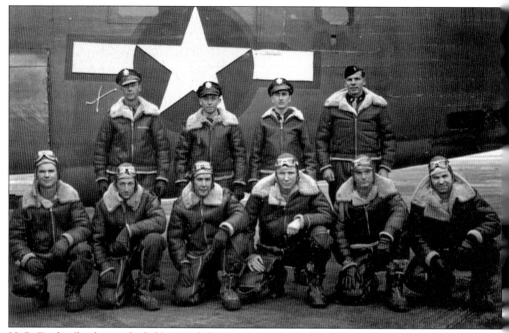

H. B. Drake (back row, far left) joined the army on August 21, 1941, and was eventually accepted into flight school at Fort Sumner, New Mexico. On April 30, 1944, H. B. and his crew were off to Tunis, Tunisia, as part of the 512th Squadron 376th Bomber Group. Later when flying out of Italy, their B-24 Liberator was shot down over Bratislava, Czechoslovakia on June 16, 1944. H. B. and seven of his crewmen were killed. (Courtesy of Jeff Miller.)

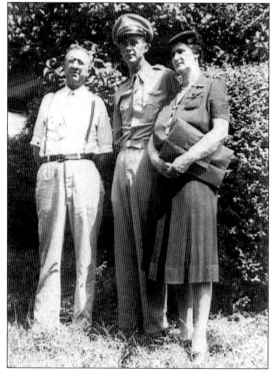

Posing in front of their home on Church Street in the early 1940s are from left to right H. E. Drake; his son, Harold Bertram Drake; and wife, Armilda Revis Drake. (Courtesy of Jeff Miller.)

Photographed here are two local boys at war. Bill Stokes of the army and Pat Flanagan of the navy bump into each other outside the Red Cross office in Casablanca, Morocco. After the war, Pat came home to work in the family printing business and Bill was the director of the city's water and sewer department. (Courtesy of Patricia F. Sproles.)

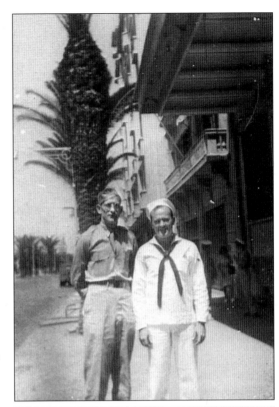

This photograph shows Mrs. M. S. McCarson receiving the Purple Heart posthumously for her son, Staff Sgt. Alvin McCarson who was killed in action over Italy. Sergeant McCarson served as a bombardier in a B-25 Mitchell bomber. During World War II, JCPenney's on Main Street kept a list in their front window of the names of local boys in the armed forces. (Courtesy of Jo Ann Stepp Fain.)

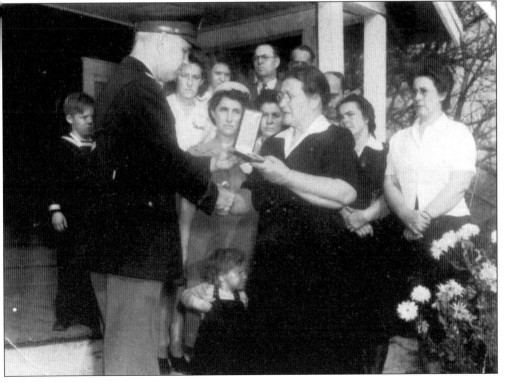

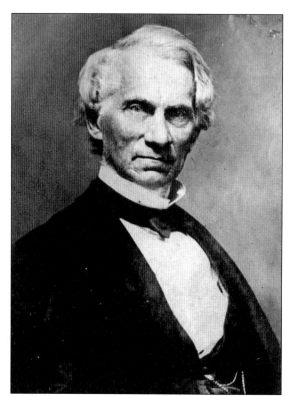

Shown here is a portrait of C. G. Memminger, first secretary of the Confederate treasury. Toward the end of the Civil War, he suggested to Pres. Jefferson Davis that the capitol be moved here. Legend has it that the president thought highly enough of the suggestion that he sent the Great Seal to Flat Rock. Before the change could take place, the war ended and the seal is thought to be buried on Glassy Mountain. Its exact location died with C. R. Memminger. (Courtesy of Carl Sandburg Home, National Historic Site, National Park Service.)

This is Edward Read Memminger, 17th child and youngest son of C. G. Memminger. Edward built his home, Tranquility, as a gift for his bride around 1890 on Little River Road on land that was the site of the Civil War story *Seven Months a Prisoner*. Edward Read was an avid plantsman. Upon his death, 1,000 specimens were given to the University of North Carolina. (Courtesy of Carl Sandburg Home, National Historic Site, National Park Service)

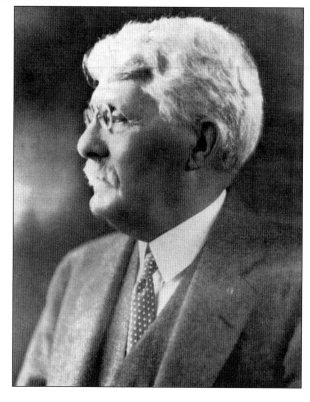

Pictured here in his army uniform during World War II is John Fanning Drake, a Hendersonville native. He served three tours of duty, one in World War II in Germany and two in Vietnam. (Courtesy of Ellen H. Drake.)

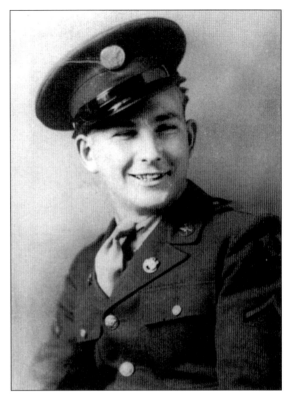

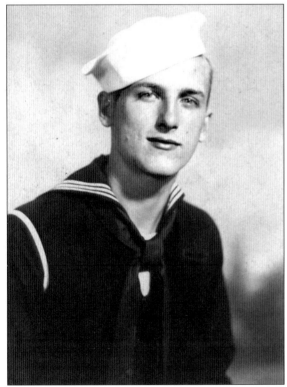

Pictured in his World War II navy uniform is Charley Edward Drake, son of Fanning and Mitchell J. Drake. He was sent into Japan right after the Japanese surrender and served on the sister ship of the *Underhill*. (Courtesy of Ellen H. Drake.)

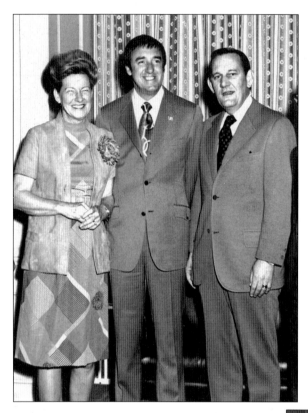

Shown here from left to right are Ophelia Calley (also known as Minnie Pearl), Jim Nabors, and David W. Cooley. Minnie Pearl and Jim Nabors were great friends. She had her first show-business experience at the Skyland Hotel where she was trained as an actress for the Sewell Company, a producer of community plays. Minnie Pearl's sister lived in Hendersonville at the time. (Courtesy of David W. Cooley.)

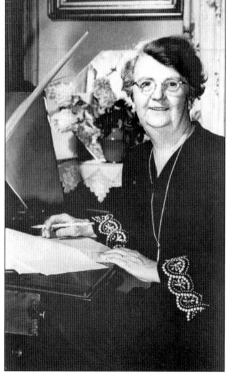

This is Sadie Smathers Patton, author of the first book on Henderson County published in 1947. Married to Preston Fidelia Patton, Sadie was a prolific author, researcher, and philanthropist. Among her many donations were 148 acres for Blue Ridge Community College and 20 acres for the first municipal park.

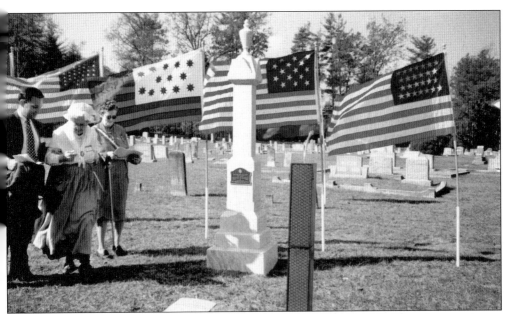

This recent image shows the gravestone of Capt. Abraham Kuykendall. The photograph was taken during dedication ceremonies sponsored by the Abraham Kuykendall Chapter of the Daughters of the American Revolution and the Kuykendall family. The grave is the oldest known in Mud Creek Church cemetery. Buried c. 1812, Captain Kuykendall was a Revolutionary War hero who received a land grant for his valiant service. He donated land for Mud Creek Church. (Courtesy of Charles Kuykendall.)

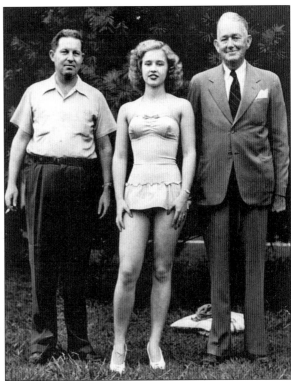

Seen here in 1948 is the queen of the Apple Harvest Festival, Juanita Thompson, daughter of Mr. and Mrs. Glenn Thompson. She married M. K. Sinclair, who went into business with the Thompson family at Seventh Avenue Produce. From left to right are Bill Freeze (who was with the *Times-News* at the time), Juanita Thompson, and G. C. "Buddy" Richardson, a local businessman. (Photograph by Horace Mann and courtesy of Hendersonville Chamber of Commerce.)

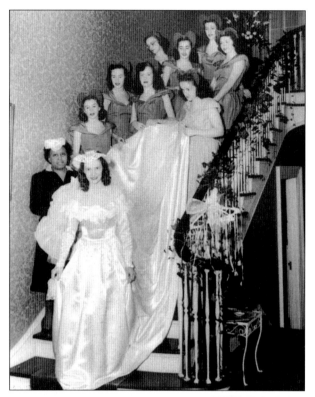

Pictured on the staircase of her family home at 1230 Fifth Avenue West, now Mélange Bed and Breakfast, Sara Buchanan poses with her wedding party. From left to right going up the stairs are Sara Buchanan, Hattie Wright (who worked for the Buchanan family), Katherine Durham, Pearl Buchanan, Jean Buchanan, four unidentified attendants, and Ann Peterson (at the top of the stairs). (Courtesy of Jean Buchanan.)

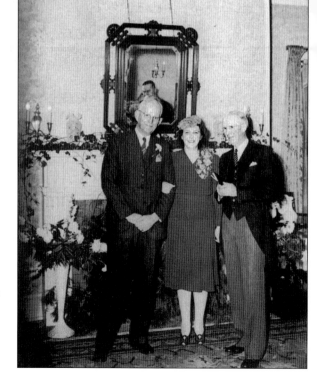

Shown here at their wedding are (from left to right) Hickman Carter, Mayme Lange, and Reverend Dr. Comack from the First Methodist Church. The house is now the Mélange Bed and Breakfast. (Courtesy of Jean Buchanan.)

This is one of the early boarders at Immaculata Catholic School, c. 1928. Lucille Vaillancourt pushes her doll carriage along the driveway at the school, which was then located on Oakland Street. (Courtesy of Immaculata Catholic School.)

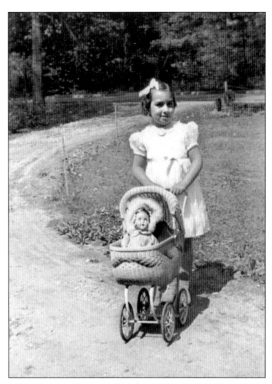

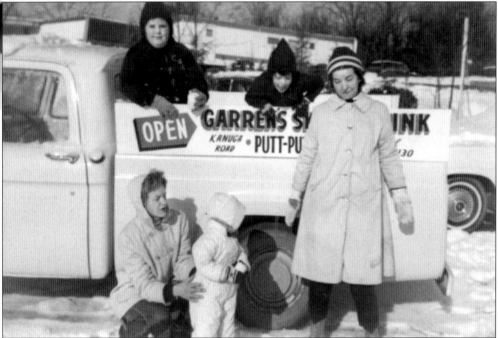

This 1950 photograph shows from left to right Freida Creasman and her daughters Debbie and Tunnie Garren. In the truck are Cathy and Judy Ellington. This truck was often used to pull floats in downtown parades and advertises the Garren's roller skating rink located on Kanuga Road. (Courtesy of Elizabeth Garren Ellington.)

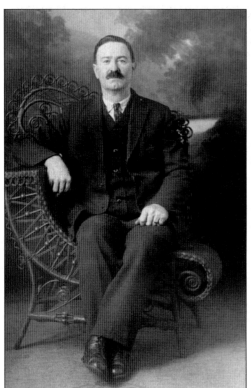

Here is a formal portrait of Glover T. Orr. He was in the transfer and livery business in Hendersonville, while his wife ran the Pine Hurst Inn on Grove Street. He became a policeman around 1929 and served as a desk sergeant until his death in 1936. (Courtesy of Barbara Peace Lohman.)

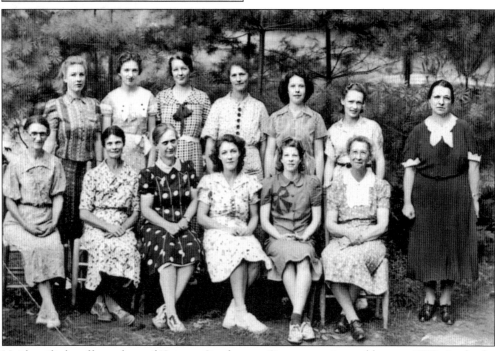

Unidentified staff members of Kanuga Conference Center are pictured here, c. 1930. At the far right is Jula Betty Drake, head housekeeper at Kanuga Conference Center. She never married and devoted her life to her family and Kanuga. (Courtesy of Deborah Summey.)

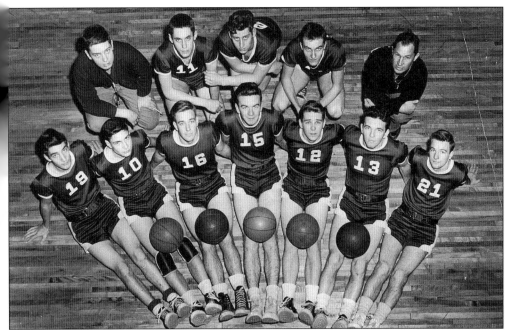

This is a picture of the "Hilltopper" basketball team of 1951 from the Blue Ridge School for Boys. From left to right are the following: (first row) George Anthony, ? Lackey, unidentified, Tommy Smith, ? Webb, Dan Case, ? Moore; (second row) unidentified, ? Pugh, ? McCombs, Moffitt Ware, and an unidentified assistant coach. Dan Case and Tommy Smith were the only local day students on the team. Most students boarded and were from all around the country. Blue Ridge School for Boys stood where the Blue Ridge Mall is today. (Courtesy of Hendersonville Chamber of Commerce.)

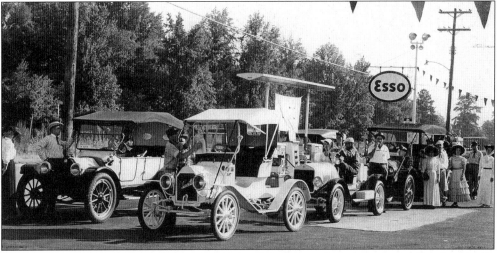

Collecting and showing antique cars has always been a popular past time for Hendersonville residents. Pictured here dressed in period costume is a group of antique car buffs about to go on parade. They appear to have just gassed up at a local Esso pump. When Jimmy Carter was president, his brother, Billy, came to town for one of Hendersonville's antique car parades. He was quite an interesting and amusing spectator and from all accounts, a very knowledgeable one. (Courtesy of Hendersonville Chamber of Commerce.)

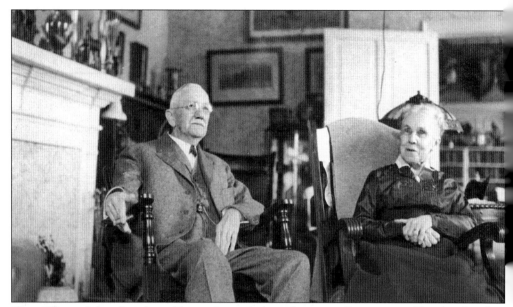

Capt. Ellison Adger Smyth and his wife are shown relaxing at Connemara. Shortly after they moved here, Captain Smyth built Balfour Mills. When local banks failed at the beginning of the Depression, Captain Smyth, with G. B. Hill and R. C. Clarke, provided the capital to organize State Trust Co., which later became the Northwestern Bank. Captain Smyth is buried in Oakdale cemetery. (Photograph from the Julianne Heggoy collection; courtesy of Carl Sandburg Home, National Historic Site, National Park Service.)

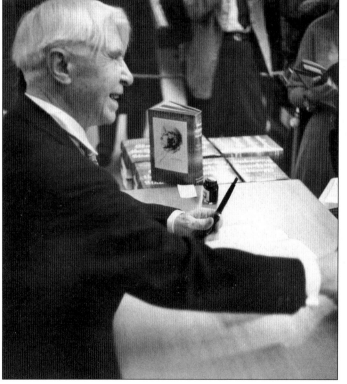

Pictured here is Carl Sandburg signing his autobiography, *Always the Young Stranger*, published in 1953. This area has always attracted artists. Carl Sandburg is best known for his six-volume biography of Lincoln. Others of note who lived or stayed here were Glen Tucker, historian and White House reporter (*Dawn Like Thunder*), Ernie Frankel (*Band of Brothers*), F. Scott Fitzgerald (*Tender is the Night*, *The Great Gatsby*), Dubose Heyward and George Gershwin (*Porgy and Bess*), and Robert Morgan (*Gap Creek*), to name just a few. (Courtesy of Carl Sandburg Home, National Historic Site, National Park Service.)

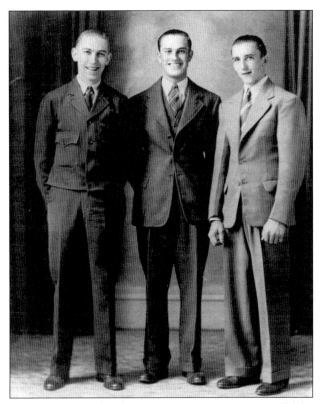

This photograph shows the Shipman Brothers. From left to right are Cliff, Buddy, and Jimmy. In the Brooks Building on the corner of Third Avenue and Church Street, Cliff ran Clifton's Restaurant while Buddy and Jimmy ran the Smoke Shop. (Courtesy of Eddie Shipman.)

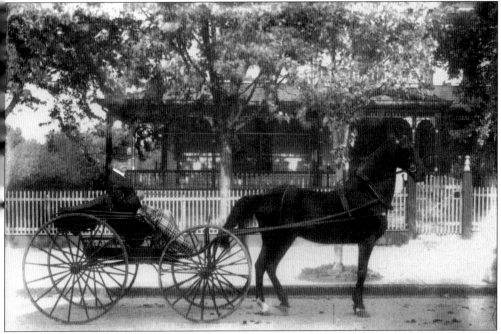

Before the Skyland Hotel was built, this house stood in its place. Dr. W. Hicks Justus is shown here, perhaps on his way to a house call. (Photograph courtesy of Charlie King; Baker-Barber Collection, Community Foundation of Henderson County.)

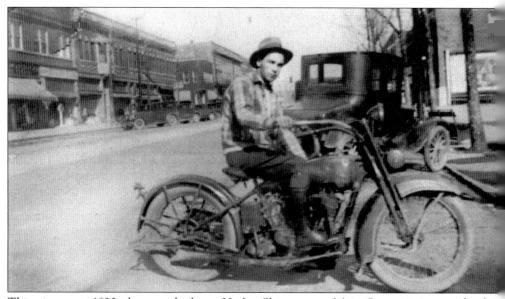

This vintage c. 1930 photograph shows Harley Shipman on Main Street sitting on the first Harley-Davidson motorcycle in Hendersonville. At this time, Shipman Motors was located on Seventh Avenue. (Courtesy of Eddie Shipman.)

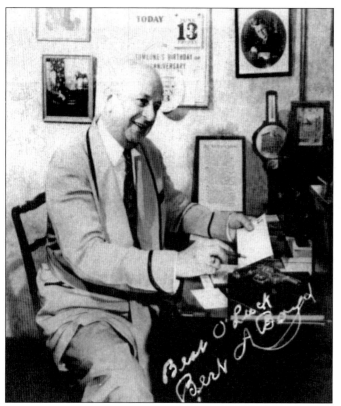

Pictured here is one of the best-loved gentlemen of his day, Bert A. Boyd, who loved the number 13. "Lucky 13er" became wealthy as a grain broker in Indianapolis and retired to Hendersonville after the death of his wife. He was a great philanthropist and dearly loved his adopted city. He donated money for tennis courts, a concession stand, and landscaping for the park that would become known as Boyd Park. (Courtesy of Jean Buchanan.)

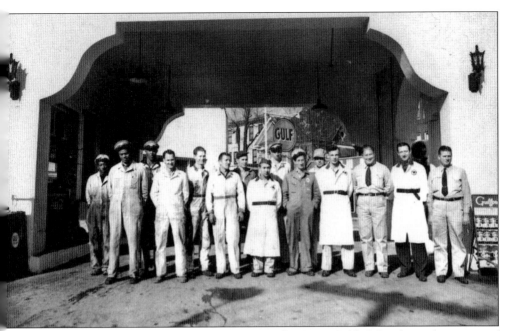

Pictured here is Boyd's Gulf Service, begun c. 1932 by Cam "Bubba" Boyd, on the corner of Church Street and Fourth Avenue. Today the business is the area's most successful General Motors dealership. Located on Route 25 North at Five Points, it is owned by L. Cam Boyd Jr. Although most people in this photograph are unidentified, the three men on the far right are, from left to right Jack Stewart, Raymond English, and Cam Boyd Sr. (Courtesy of L. Cam Boyd Jr.)

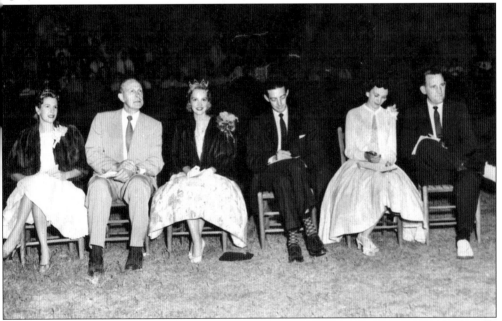

People in this photograph are Don Barber (in the light colored suit), noted Hendersonville photographer, and David W. Cooley (on the far right) with three unidentified ladies and one gentleman. They were judging a Miss North Carolina beauty pageant. (Courtesy of David W. Cooley.)

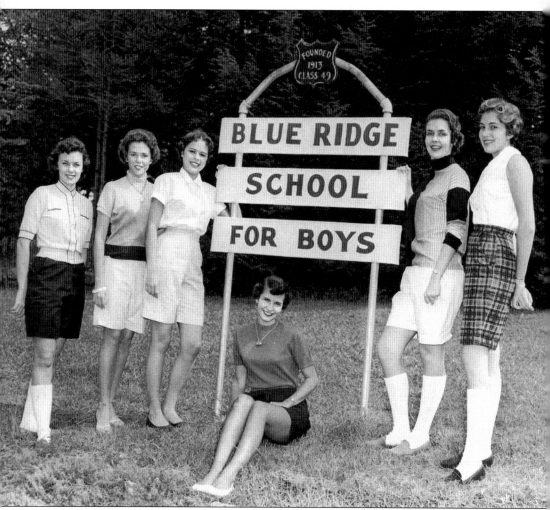

This image relates to another Hendersonville mystery. During the research for this book, authors were given plenty of knowledge concerning this wonderful city. But it seemed for every question answered, two more would emerge. Some examples include the following: Who are these young ladies, and why are they hanging around the entrance to the Blue Ridge School for Boys? Were the best hamburgers served at Brocks or the Hasty Tasty? Why did "The Underground" shops, located below the street on the northwest corner of Main and Fourth Streets, close? Where could you get the best barbeque, Shorty's Pig and Whistle or Johnny's? As a senior prank, did a group really manage to get one of Johnny Mitchell's bulls up to the third floor of Hendersonville High School, and how did they get the bull down? Was Mrs. Morgan of the Teen Canteen as tough a chaperone as people say? Did the *Newlywed Game* in Hollywood really reward their winning couple with a trip to the Apple Festival in Hendersonville? And what really went on at Tracy's next to the bus station?